Learning through Literature

Fun Language Arts Activities with a Science Twist

by
Jackie Carpas
Melissa Hughes
Caroline Lenzo
Kristin Oakes

illustrations by
Ray Lambert

Carson-Dellosa Publishing Company, Inc.

Greensboro, North Carolina

Credits

Editors: Debra Olson Pressnall, Louise Vaughn, Karen Seberg
Cover and Inside Illustrations: Ray Lambert
Cover Production: Annette Hollister-Papp
Text Production: Louise Vaughn, Mark Conrad

© 2004 Carson-Dellosa Publishing Company, Inc., Greensboro, North Carolina 27424. The purchase of this material entitles the buyer to reproduce worksheets and activities for classroom use only—not for commercial resale. Reproduction of these materials for an entire school or district is prohibited. No part of this book may be reproduced (except as noted above), stored in a retrieval system, or transmitted in any form or by any means (mechanically, electronically, recording, etc.) without the prior written consent of Carson-Dellosa Publishing Co., Inc.

Printed in the USA • All rights reserved.

ISBN 0-88724-260-X

Table of Contents

Introduction 4
  Reading Strategies 4
  Assessments 5
  Parent Communication 5
  KWL Chart Reproducible 6
  Student Evaluation Forms 7
  Open Grading Chart 8

Bears and Other Mammals 9
  Literature Selections 10
  Language Arts 14
  Author Ideas 16
  Art, Music & Drama 17
  Fun Recipes 19
  Math 21
  At-Home Activities 23

Dinosaurs 27
  Literature Selections 28
  Language Arts 31
  Author Ideas 37
  Art, Music & Drama 38
  Fun Recipes 41
  Math 42
  At-Home Activities 44

Frogs and Other Amphibians 47
  Literature Selections 48
  Language Arts 51
  Author Ideas 57
  Art, Music & Drama 60
  Fun Recipes 65
  Math 66
  At-Home Activities 67

Insects and Spiders 69
  Literature Selections 70
  Language Arts 72
  Author Ideas 79
  Art, Music & Drama 82
  Fun Recipes 85
  Math 86
  At-Home Activities 87

My Body 89
  Literature Selections 90
  Language Arts 92
  Author Ideas 96
  Art, Music & Drama 100
  Fun Recipes 103
  Math 104
  At-Home Activities 106

Plants and Trees 111
  Literature Selections 112
  Language Arts 115
  Author Ideas 119
  Art, Music & Drama 122
  Fun Recipes 124
  Math 125
  At-Home Activities 127

Introduction

Young children are naturally curious about the world around them. They ask questions and explore, as well as collect, sort, and build things. All of these early childhood developmental skills can also be associated with science process skills. Teachers who have developed successful science programs enable students to see science concepts everywhere.

One method teachers use to engage their students in science topics is by introducing good quality literature. Literature can reinforce, illustrate, and connect science concepts in ways that textbooks cannot. Intriguing stories, fascinating pictures, interesting characters, and various means of expression bring science to life and can become springboards for classroom discussions and inquiry-based explorations. Fiction, nonfiction, poetry, and picture books can all inspire students to investigate science in personally meaningful ways. Incorporating rich literature selections into your science program is an exciting way to engage the natural scientist in every child while fostering the development of language arts and reading skills.

Learning through Literature is designed to provide teachers with science-based ideas and activities that can be integrated with a language arts curriculum. From frogs and other amphibians to bears and other mammals, you'll be delighted at how easily you can adapt each lesson to meet specific science objectives. Each chapter theme begins with a concept map illustrating the language arts activities, fun recipes, author ideas, and at-home activities that support a life science topic. Pre-reading, guided reading, and post-reading strategies also help teachers assess students' prior knowledge, foster inquiry-based learning, invite students to question and learn more, and generate cross-curricular learning experiences.

Reading Strategies

Pre-reading strategies offer teachers a chance to "hook" their students on science topics. Before beginning an activity, introduce the literature selection by reading aloud the title and author of the book and showing the book cover. Then ask your students to explain how they think the book applies to the current unit of study. Encouraging students to make predictions and ask questions before reading a selection are good ways to assess what they already know and stimulate interest. Another effective tool, the use of a KWL (<u>K</u>now, <u>W</u>ant to know, <u>L</u>earned) chart helps students organize background knowledge of the subject and sheds light on any misconceptions they may have. (See page 6 for a KWL chart reproducible.)

Guided reading strategies incorporate the reinforcement of scientific concepts and stimulate further inquiry. Perhaps students have science questions about something that occurs in the story. These class discussions can act as a springboard for hands-on investigations. Providing opportunities for students to identify new vocabulary words in context, main ideas, and details as they read are also effective methods to support science instruction. Graphic organizers, such as Venn diagrams, can be used to help students record important information they find in literature. (See pages 35 and 56 for Venn diagram reproducibles.) Guided reading strategies provide students with a lens through which to "look" at the literature selections.

Post-reading strategies encourage students to explore new ideas and raise questions as they synthesize information and acknowledge a connection between the literature selection and scientific concepts. This book contains a variety of language arts activities, such as sequencing and research reports, to give students a chance to reflect on their learning and respond critically. Art, music, and drama activities can also be effective ways to allow kinesthetic learners demonstrate new knowledge through role-playing, art, and song. Post-reading strategies use the literature selections as a bridge for hands-on, inquiry-based activities in which students will be engaged.

Assessment

As teachers, we all want our students to enjoy learning. Creating art projects, writing poetry, and role-playing stories can all be fun for students. However, some teachers find it difficult to assess student learning in these kinds of activities. We have included two assessment tools to assist both teachers and students in defining clear learning expectations and for monitoring the mastery of skills. An example of an open grading chart is shown on the bottom of page 8. This type of chart can be modified to measure student learning in the form of pupil performance outcomes or learning goals. Fill in the first column with the goals or objectives of the activity. Share the grading criteria with students as you introduce the assignment to define your expectations clearly. You could also create the grading criteria together as a class. In this way, students are focused on the objectives of the project and actively involved in establishing high standards for quality work. Make sure you keep the goals clear and concise and use language that students understand. Student evaluation forms (see pages 7 and 8) are effective tools for students to monitor their own progress on projects and evaluate areas of weakness.

Parent Communication

Communicating clear expectations to parents is especially important at the primary level. Many parents want to be involved in their children's education, but do not know how to help. Some teachers have found that parents are more willing to participate in at-home activities with their children when they receive information (perhaps in the form of a classroom newsletter) about a particular science unit prior to students studying the topic in class. If parents know in advance that you'll be studying insects, for example, they can easily facilitate interest in that topic by taking a trip to the local library or investigating related Web sites with their children. Furthermore, parents can provide additional resources such as photographs, materials, and "experts" in the field (e.g., landscapers, entomologists, etc.) for your classroom learning experiences. This link between home and classroom can also be strengthened by asking parents to work with their children on special activities. Included in this resource book are at-home activities for each science theme that provide parents with opportunities to reinforce concepts and share rich literature with their children.

KWL Chart

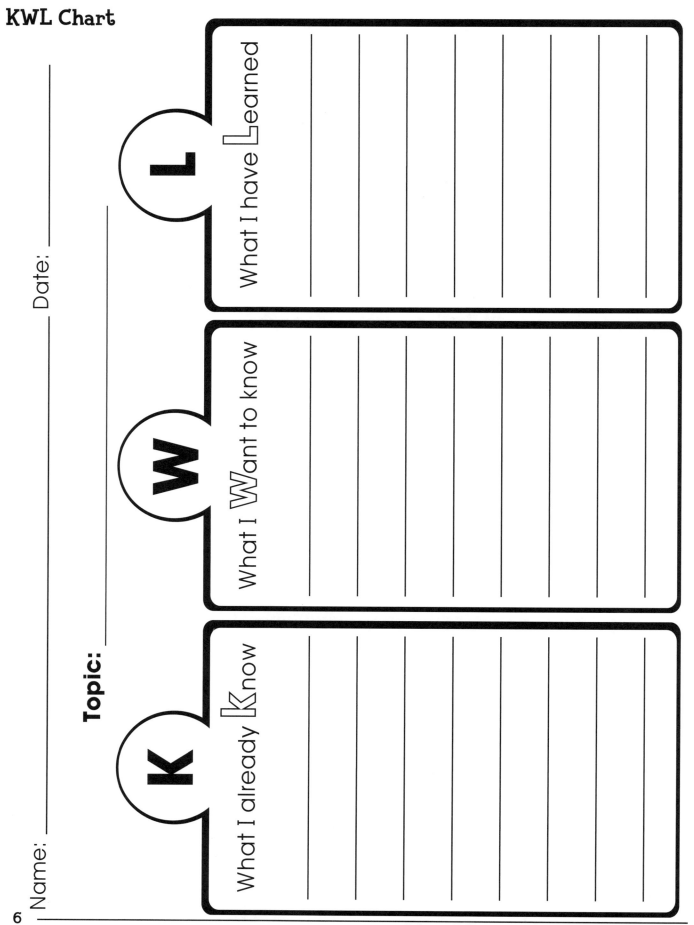

Student Evaluation Forms

Student Evaluation Form for (project) _____

Name: _____	I'm pleased	I'm disappointed
This is how I feel about my finished project:	🙂	☹️
This is how I feel about how hard I worked on my project:	🙂	☹️
I think others will feel this way when they look at my work:	🙂	☹️
I feel this way when I think about doing another project:	🙂	☹️

Name: _____ Date: _____

Student Evaluation for _____

I like my work because _____

_____

_____

Next time I want to improve _____

_____

_____

On a scale from 1 to 10, I would rate my effort on this project:

low 1 2 3 4 5 6 7 8 9 10 **high**

Student Evaluation Form/Open Grading Chart

Name:_____ Date:_____

Color the face to show how you would rate your work on the _____ project.

This is my best work.

I can do better next time.

This was not my best effort!

Project:			
Student:		Date:	
Objectives	Great Job!	Good!	Keep Working!
1.	3	2	1
2.	3	2	1
3.	3	2	1
4.	3	2	1
Total Points:			

Bears and Other Mammals

Children enjoy learning about animals. Even very young children have a great deal of knowledge on this topic from experiences with animals at the zoo as well as pets and other common animals they may encounter in their neighborhoods. Opportunities for curriculum integration are varied and many, as you can see with this concept map.

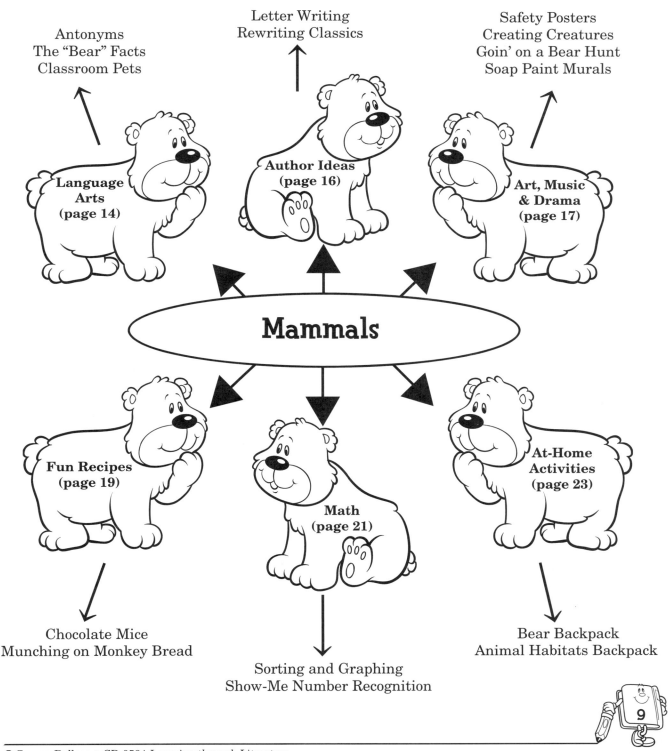

Antonyms
The "Bear" Facts
Classroom Pets

↑

Language Arts (page 14)

Letter Writing
Rewriting Classics

↑

Author Ideas (page 16)

Safety Posters
Creating Creatures
Goin' on a Bear Hunt
Soap Paint Murals

↑

Art, Music & Drama (page 17)

Mammals

Fun Recipes (page 19)

↓

Chocolate Mice
Munching on Monkey Bread

Math (page 21)

↓

Sorting and Graphing
Show-Me Number Recognition

At-Home Activities (page 23)

↓

Bear Backpack
Animal Habitats Backpack

© Carson-Dellosa • CD-0584 *Learning through Literature*

Literature Selections

Featured Literature

The following selections are used in conjunction with the activities in this section. You may want to obtain them from your library before you start the unit. (Activities with which the books are used are listed in parentheses.)

Nonfiction

Alaska's Three Bears, by Shelley Gill (Paws IV Publishing Co., 1990). Three bears—a brown bear, a black bear, and a polar bear—travel across Alaska until each finds the home for which it is best suited. The bottom of each page shares scientific facts about the bears. (The "Bear" Facts, page 14; Rewriting Classics, page 16; Safety Posters, page 17)

Children of the Earth . . . Remember, by Schim Schimmel (NorthWord Press, 1997). The author tells a story about how animals and people need to work together to protect the world they share. (Soap Paint Murals, page 18)

Dear Children of the Earth, by Schim Schimmel (NorthWord Press, 1994). A letter from Mother Earth to her children asking for help in saving Earth and its creatures is the theme of this book. (Soap Paint Murals, page 18)

The Family of Earth, by Schim Schimmel (NorthWord Press, 2001). Earth looks different to each of us depending upon where we live. The theme of the book reminds us that there is only one Earth so we must be careful to share and take care of it. (Soap Paint Murals, page 18; Animal Habitats Backpack, page 24)

Hibernation, by Carolyn Scrace (F. Watts, 2002). This book introduces hibernation by explaining all the steps a dormouse goes through as it gets ready to hibernate. (Chocolate Mice, page 19)

In the Woods: Who's Been Here? by Lindsay Barrett George (Greenwillow Books, 1995). A boy and girl go for a walk in the woods and see evidence of animal life, such as nests and cocoons, even though they do not actually see the animals. (Animal Habitats Backpack, page 24)

Fiction

Caps for Sale, by Esphyr Slobodkina (Harper & Row, 1985). A group of monkeys steals a vendor's caps while he sleeps and he must work to get them back. (Munching on Monkey Bread, page 20)

Dear Mr. Blueberry, by Simon James (Maxwell Macmillan International Pub. Group, 1991). A little girl, Emily, corresponds with her teacher about how to care for the whale in her backyard pond. Students will learn many facts about whales as you read and discuss this book. (Letter Writing, page 16)

© Carson-Dellosa • CD-0584 *Learning through Literature*

Bears and Other Mammals

Do You Want to Be My Friend? by Eric Carle (Philomel Books, 1988). A mouse goes in search of a friend. The reader receives a clue as to each potential friend's identity by first seeing the animal's tail. (Classroom Pets, page 15)

Does a Mouse Have a House? by Anne Miranda (Bradbury Press, 1994). The book tells where animals live using rhyme and colorful illustrations. (Chocolate Mice, page 19)

Five Little Monkeys Jumping on the Bed, by Eileen Christelow (Clarion Books, 1989). Five little monkeys jump on the bed until one by one, they all fall off and their mother puts them to bed. (Munching on Monkey Bread, page 20)

I Love You with All My Heart, by Noris Kern (Chronicle Books, 2002). A polar bear cub talks to his animal friends to see how their mothers demonstrate love for them. He finishes his day talking to his mother about all the ways she shows her love for him. (Bear Backpack, page 23)

The Kissing Hand, by Audrey Penn (Child Welfare League of America, 1993). A mother raccoon helps her son overcome his fear of separation by teaching him about the kissing hand. (Bear Backpack, page 23)

No Matter What, by Debi Gliori (Harcourt Brace, 1999). The reader learns how Large reassures Small that he is loved no matter what. (Bear Backpack, page 23)

The Opposites, by Monique Felix (Creative Education, 1992). A brown mouse and a white mouse demonstrate opposites in this book with the use of pictures instead of words. (Antonyms, page 14)

The Three Little Pigs and ***Goldilocks and the Three Bears*** —any traditional version. (Rewriting Classics, page 16)

We're Going on a Bear Hunt, retold by Michael Rosen (Aladdin Books, 1992). The story line describes the adventures a family experiences as they hunt for a bear. (Goin' on a Bear Hunt, page 17)

Additional Suggested Literature

Nonfiction

Animals & Art Activities, by Janet Sacks (Crabtree Publishing Co., 2002). This book offers a number of art projects featuring animals.

Animalia, by Graeme Base (Harry N. Abrams, Inc., 1987). This beautifully illustrated animal alphabet book uses alliteration to describe each animal.

The Bear Under the Stairs, by Helen Cooper (Dial Books for Young Readers, 1993) A little boy keeps feeding the bear he thinks lives under the stairs and his mother helps him overcome his fear.

The Berenstain Bears' Big Book of Science and Nature, by Stan and Jan Berenstain (Random House, 1997). This resource is full of fascinating facts about our world and contains simple science experiments.

Bears and Other Mammals

Gone Forever! An Alphabet of Extinct Animals, by Sandra and William Markle (Atheneum Books for Young Readers, 1998). This alphabet book focuses on animals that have become extinct since the days of the dinosaur.

Hey Daddy! Animal Fathers and Their Babies, by Mary Batten (Peachtree, 2002). This book illustrates the many ways that dads, both animal and human, help to raise their babies.

If You Were Born a Kitten, by Marion Dane Bauer (Simon and Schuster Books for Young Readers, 1997). This book describes how animal babies and humans come into the world.

In November, by Cynthia Rylant (Harcourt Brace, 2000). The authors tells about what happens in November as animals and people get ready for winter.

Over in the Meadow, illustrated by Ezra Jack Keats (Viking, 1971). This traditional poem uses poetry to introduce animals and their young as well as counting from one to ten.

Polar Bear, Polar Bear, What Do You Hear? by Bill Martin, Jr., and Eric Carle (Henry Holt, 1991). The sounds that animals make are featured in this book.

Prairie Dogs Kiss and Lobsters Wave: How Animals Say Hello, by Marilyn Singer (Holt, 1998). The book tells how 14 different animals say hello to each other.

Mammals, by Barbara Taylor (Kingfisher, 2002). A good classroom reference book, young readers will enjoy the interesting photos, illustrations, and facts about mammals.

Who Hops? by Katie Davis (Harcourt Brace, 1998). Each section of this book lists animals that move in the same way. The section ends with an animal that does not fit in with the group but then tells children what that animal can do.

Who Is in the Garden? by Vera Rosenberry (Holiday House, 2001). A boy takes a walk in a garden and meets many of its animal inhabitants.

Who Says Moo? by Ruth Young (Viking, 1994). There are questions and answers in this book about animals. The illustrations help children answer questions about animals' appearances, the way they move, and the sounds they make.

Fiction

Cows Can't Fly, by David Milgrim (Viking, 1998). This book uses rhyme to tell about a boy who tries to convince those around him that cows can fly.

Does a Kangaroo Have a Mother Too? by Eric Carle (Harper Collins, 2000). The author uses repetition to ask if each of a dozen animals has a mother and helps answer the questions with illustrations of the mothers with their babies. The end of the book reveals the name of the baby, parent, and group of each animal.

Bears and Other Mammals

Eric Carle's Animals, Animals, illustrated by Eric Carle (Philomel Books, 1989). Eric Carle's distinctive artwork brings to life animal poetry written by various poets.

If You Give a Mouse a Cookie, by Laura Numeroff (Harper & Row, 1985). A mouse makes many demands after a boy gives him a cookie.

I Had a Cat, by Mona Rabun Reeves (Bradbury Press, 1989). In this story, a girl has many, many animals, but then runs out of food and has to give them all away, except for her cat.

The Mitten: A Ukrainian Folktale, adapted and illustrated by Jan Brett (Putnam, 1989). Woodland animals find Micki's snow-white mitten and use it to keep warm.

The Mouse and the Motorcycle, by Beverly Cleary (William Morrow & Co., 1965). This is the story of a mouse and his beloved motorcycle and the many adventures that he has.

Nuts to You, by Lois Ehlert (Harcourt Brace Jovanovich., 1993). A squirrel befriends a child who shares nuts with it. The back of the book discloses many facts about the characteristics and habits of squirrels.

Off We Go, by Jane Yolen (Little, Brown, 2000). This beautifully illustrated book tells how the baby woodland animals make their way to Grandma's.

Runaway Ralph, by Beverly Cleary (HarperTrophy, 1991). This book relates many humorous adventures of Ralph, the mouse, on his motorcycle.

Stuart Little, by E. B. White (HarperCollins, 1974). A mouse is adopted by humans.

Language Arts

Antonyms

Literature: *The Opposites*, by Monique Felix

Activity: *The Opposites*, Monique Felix's book about two adorable mice, one brown and one white, is a great way to introduce or reinforce antonyms with your class. The book has no words, just pictures of the two mice doing "opposite" things like going up or down the stairs or going in or out of the door. Children will benefit from the opportunity to practice their language skills as they describe the mice and their antics.

The last page of the book shows the color fading from the brown mouse, which then presents you with the opportunity to retell the story using synonyms. Be sure to write the synonym and antonym pairs on the board or on a chart so that you can easily review them.

You may want students to draw pictures to be incorporated into classroom books about synonyms and antonyms. It will not be too time consuming if each child contributes one page to the class effort.

The "Bear" Facts

Literature: *Alaska's Three Bears*, by Shelley Gill

Materials: Overheard projector, butcher paper (brown, black, and white), markers, measuring stick or tape measure, light color paint pen or chalk (optional)

Activity: Shelley Gill's book *Alaska's Three Bears* is almost like reading two books in one. The story at the top of each page, illustrated by Shannon Cartwright, tells about the adventures of three bears—a white bear, a brown bear, and a black bear—as they walk through the wilderness looking for a suitable home. The bottom of each page is full of factual information about bears that you can share with the class.

Use the information from this book to create a "Bear" Facts bulletin board in your classroom. Using your overhead projector and the measurements given in the book, trace each of the bears, life size, on the appropriate color of butcher paper. Write, "Did you know that . . . ?" on the appropriate bear. (Use a white or other light color paint pen or chalk to write on the dark-colored bears, or write the questions on paper and then post them on the bears.) As you reread the facts from the book, record important specific information right on each bear. Divide the class into groups to decorate and cut out the bears. Mount the bears on a wall in your classroom or in the hallway. The display will serve as a constant reminder of what the class has learned about their furry friends and will allow students to see just how huge these animals are.

Bears and Other **Mammals**

Classroom Pets

Literature: *Do You Want to Be My Friend?* by Eric Carle (Optional: *Runaway Ralph*, by Beverly Cleary; *The Mouse and the Motorcycle*, by Beverly Cleary; *Stuart Little*, by E. B. White; *If You Give a Mouse a Cookie*, by Laura Numeroff)

Materials: Pet mouse or mice, cage or old aquarium, water bottle or dish, wood shavings, cotton or batting, cardboard toilet paper tubes, and food; videotape of *Stuart Little* or *Runaway Ralph* and cheese popcorn or cheese balls

Activity: Read *Do You Want to Be My Friend?* by Eric Carle, about a mouse who is searching for a friend. As you discuss the book, talk about the characteristics that make a mouse a mammal: it has fur, is warm blooded, gives birth to live young, and so on.

Consider adopting a mouse as a classroom pet. Research and gather the things that you will need to create a habitat for a mouse, such as a cage or old aquarium, water bottle or dish, wood shavings, cotton or batting, cardboard toilet paper tubes, and food. Parents may be willing to donate these items or you may be able to find them in a storeroom in your building. The nice thing about mice is that they are not too particular about their living conditions!

When you visit the pet store to purchase your mouse, you may want to buy two or three so that they can keep each other company. If you would like to observe their life cycle, obtain mice of both genders. If you do not want the mice to reproduce, make sure to get mice of the same gender. Don't worry about overpopulation. You can find homes for the extra mice by giving them to students who bring in a signed permission slip from their parents or you can trade the mice back to the pet store for food or bedding supplies.

Some activities and things to think about concerning your classroom pet:

- Arrange for a student to take the pet home during school breaks and holidays.

- Give students an opportunity to earn the privilege of reading to the pet.

- Create a mouse library by collecting books about mice from your classroom library, the school library, or the local library or by having children bring in donations.

- Make time to read with your class some classic stories about mice. (See list shown above.)

- As a class treat for good behavior, show the movie *Runaway Ralph* or *Stuart Little* to the class. Don't forget the cheese popcorn or cheese balls!

- Make cleaning the mouse house a job for students. Believe it or not, you will probably find at least one of your students or perhaps an older student helper who would love to have this responsibility. Make sure that you provide a supply of disposable gloves for this job!

- Create an ongoing "Mouse Facts" bulletin board to record all of the things your class learns about mice throughout the year. You may want to display a picture of a mouse and record the facts on paper shaped like pieces of cheese.

Author Ideas

Letter Writing

Literature: *Dear Mr. Blueberry*, by Simon James

Activity: Reading *Dear Mr. Blueberry*, by Simon James, will help you introduce letter writing to your class. This is a book about a child who writes to her teacher to get information about the whale that showed up in her backyard pond. Talk with your students about how writing letters can be a good way to communicate with another person. Make a list of the people to whom your class could write to gather information about animals. Your list might include a veterinarian, animal control officer, park ranger, zoo worker, dog trainer, dog groomer, breeder, farmer, or blacksmith.

To begin the activity, you might want to choose one or two people with whom to correspond and then work with the class to develop a letter before having your students write independently. Be sure to stress the importance of incorporating all of the parts of a letter: date, greeting, body, closing, and signature. Mail the letters and wait for a response.

Make letter-writing assignments more meaningful by having students write letters of invitation to their parents, speakers, or guest readers. Follow up each visit with a thank-you note.

Children also love to receive mail. Encourage them to design and illustrate their own postcards with pictures of animals they have studied. They could be used to recommend a favorite book or to share animal facts with a classmate or pen pal in a neighboring room. Use classroom mailboxes to distribute mail to students. The more practice your students have writing formal and informal letters, the more proficient they will become.

Variation: Have the students compose letters to authors of their favorite books, telling them how much they like their work and asking them questions about the books. Many authors have Web sites that you can visit to find out more or E-mail addresses that you can use to communicate with them.

Rewriting Classics

Literature: *Alaska's Three Bears*, by Shelley Gill; "The Three Little Pigs" (any traditional version in story form or book), "Goldilocks and the Three Bears" (any traditional version in story form or book)

Activity: After reading the classic stories "The Three Little Pigs" and "Goldilocks and the Three Bears," read *Alaska's Three Bears,* by Shelley Gill, to your class. As a group or individually, have the students create new versions of the classics by making the main characters a brown bear, a black bear, and a white bear. What adventures will they have? Whom will they meet along the way? Whom will the villain be? (Perhaps humans! How might humans endanger the environment and the bears' way of life?) How can the conflict be resolved?

Art, Music & Drama

Bears and Other Mammals

Safety Posters

Literature: *Alaska's Three Bears*, by Shelley Gill

Materials: Crayons, markers, or chalk; drawing paper; pencils

Activity: At the end of her book, *Alaska's Three Bears,* Shelley Gill, talks about ways to be safe around bears. Spend some time with your class discussing how these pointers could help keep them safe around other animals as well. Students may want to share other rules that they have learned. Record them on the board or on a chart. Have each student choose a rule or suggestion to illustrate on a poster. You may want to display their works of art on a bulletin board or in the hallway.

Creating Creatures

Literature: Several factual animal books

Materials: Modeling clay or materials to make papier-mâché, tempera paint and brushes (if not using colored clay)

Activity: Children may enjoy creating their favorite mammals using clay or papier-mâché. After reading several animal books to the class, have the students choose animals that they would like to make. Perhaps your building has a kiln where the clay creatures can be fired and glazed. If not, use clay that can air dry to harden. If you cannot allow time for the children to paint their creations, have them work with colored clay. Give each child a lump of clay and let the fun begin as students create their favorite mammals.

Students may want to create habitats for their animals by making trioramas (see page 40 for directions). Alternatively, students could display their animals in peep boxes or dioramas.

Have children gather facts about their animals. They can then use their models as props as they make oral reports to the class about their favorite mammals.

Goin' on a Bear Hunt

Literature: *We're Going on a Bear Hunt*, retold by Michael Rosen

Activity: *We're Going on a Bear Hunt,* by Michael Rosen, illustrates and tells the tale of a family that goes in search of bears. Many of your students will be familiar with this selection and will quickly join in as you read the story thanks to its repetitive pattern. Have the students form small groups and then think of ways to act out the story.

If you are planning to invite parents or another class to visit your room, this selection would be easy for the class to perform. You may choose to use props or hand motions to enhance the story.

Bears and Other Mammals

Soap Paint Murals

Literature: *Children of the Earth . . . Remember*, by Schim Schimmel; *Dear Children of the Earth*, by Schim Schimmel; *The Family of Earth*, by Schim Schimmel

Materials: Soap paint in a variety of colors (see recipe below), brushes, long sheet of butcher paper, paint shirts or smocks, colored art sand (optional), glitter (optional)

Activity: Students are sure to enjoy all three of the books written by Schim Schimmel—*Children of the Earth . . . Remember, Dear Children of the Earth,* and *The Family of Earth*—which tell how animals and humans share the earth and depend on each other to take care of it properly. The illustrations in these books are beautiful and are likely to hold your students' attention. Why not take advantage of their interest by having them create a mural that shares the message of this author? One way that you could do this is by making soap paint. It will put a little twist into painting and should add dimension to the students' creations. Here's how:

Create a center or special area in your classroom for students to work and where needed supplies are readily available. After reading the books by Schim Schimmel, have small groups of students take turns visiting the center to paint their favorite parts of the books. You may want to divide the paper into three sections—sky, land, and sea—so that students will be sure to include something from each area in the mural. Display the finished project on a bulletin board or in the hallway. Art sand and glitter could add just the right touch to set off this work of art.

Variations: If you do not feel like taking on a project as large as a mural, you could have students work on individual pictures at their desks or at a center. These works could be displayed individually or taped together in a quilt design to make a bigger impact.

Do not hesitate to ask for help: Your school's art teacher may be willing to incorporate this project into his regular art classes or at least share some drawing or painting techniques with your class. Ask parents to assist you by supervising the project in your art center or working with small groups of students in the hallway where they can spread out as they work.

Recipe for Soap Paint

1 c. (237 mL) soap flakes
1/2 c. (119 mL) cold water
food coloring

Pour the cold water into a bowl. Add the soap flakes and beat with a mixer until stiff (the consistency of beaten egg whites). Add food coloring and beat thoroughly. Paint on heavy paper or cardboard. Art sand and glitter may be applied to the wet paint.

Fun Recipes

Bears and Other **Mammals**

Chocolate Mice

Literature: *Does a Mouse Have a House?* by Anne Miranda; *Hibernation*, by Carolyn Scrace

Materials: Maraschino cherries with stems, milk chocolate squares, small candies for eyes, slivered almonds, mini chocolate chips, chocolate drop-shaped candy, small doilies or paper candy cups, electric skillet

Activity: After reading aloud *Does a Mouse Have a House?* by Anne Miranda, and/or *Hibernation*, by Carolyn Scrace, you could follow up with this delicious activity. As the children create chocolate mice, they will find that each mouse takes on a personality of its own. Just wait and see! Take pictures to send home or make a number of these to serve to guests on a special day. You may also want to share them with other teachers and the office staff.

Melt chocolate squares in an electric skillet. Unwrap all of the chocolate drop-shaped candy. Hold the cherries by the stems and immerse them into the warm chocolate. Set each on a doily or in a paper candy cup, with the stem pointing to side and not upright. While the chocolate is still warm, press one chocolate drop-shaped candy onto the front of the cherry to serve as the mouse's head, then place two slivered almonds between the candy and the cherry for ears. Attach candy eyes and a nose made of a mini chocolate chip by using a toothpick to place a dab of melted chocolate behind them. The cherry stem will serve as the tail.

Variation: This project might also be fun to do at Christmastime as the children read about Christmas mice in stories such as "A Visit from St. Nicholas" ("Twas the Night before Christmas") by Clement Clarke Moore. Students could make the candy mice to give as gifts to their families. Simply put the mice in small candy boxes and tie each with a ribbon. Make gift tags with the words "Not a creature was stirring . . . not even a mouse," and have students sign their names.

© Carson-Dellosa • CD-0584 *Learning through Literature*

Bears and Other Mammals

Munching on Monkey Bread

Literature: *Five Little Monkeys Jumping on the Bed*, by Eileen Christelow; *Caps for Sale*, by Esphyr Slobodkina

Materials: 3 cans refrigerated buttermilk biscuits (10 biscuits each), 1 c. (237 mL) granulated sugar, 2 tsp. (10 mL) cinnamon, 1 c. (237 mL) brown sugar, 1 stick margarine, 1 1/4 c. (296 mL) nuts (optional), saucepan, spoon, tube pan, oven, plate, large plastic bag

Activity: Decide whether you want to make monkey bread for your students or have them participate in the process. Either way, preparing and eating monkey bread will make reading the stories *Five Little Monkeys Jumping on the Bed*, by Eileen Christelow, and *Caps for Sale*, by Esphyr Slobodkina, even more fun.

Gather the materials listed above. Cut each biscuit into quarters. Shake the biscuit pieces with the cinnamon and granulated sugar in a large plastic bag. Place one layer of biscuits in the tube pan and sprinkle with nuts (if students are not allergic to nuts); repeat to make two more layers. Melt the margarine in the saucepan. Add brown sugar and boil for one minute. Pour over the biscuits and bake at 350° F (177° C) for 35 minutes. Remove the baking pan from the oven. Turn it upside down on a plate. Let cool for 10 minutes. Eat with your fingers just like a monkey!

Math

Sorting and Graphing

Materials: Chewy bear-shaped candy or math markers, reproducible (page 22), pencils, crayons

Activity: Distribute a handful of chewy bear-shaped candy and a copy of the reproducible sheet from page 22 to each child. Have the children sort the bears by color, recording the number of candies they have of each color in the correct box. Demonstrate on the overhead or at the board how they can make a graph with the results. You may also want to determine the total number of bears the class counted and then graph those results. The best part of this activity is eating the candy at the end!

Variations: Have the children make addition and subtraction math facts with the chewy candy. Examples: 3 red + 4 yellow = 7 bears, or 5 green – 1 orange = 4 bears

Each child could place a star by the color bear she likes best. Tally the class's results and make a graph to post on your door.

Show-Me Number Recognition

Materials: Bear-shaped counters or other math counters, Show-Me Cards (instructions below), overhead projector (optional)

Activity: Instruct your students to take their Show-Me cards out of the plastic bags and place them on their desks in numerical order beginning with zero. Using the cards will enable each child to respond to your questions and allow you to identify those who are struggling with the activity.

Place a number of bear-shaped counters on the overhead or draw a set on the board. Have students count them, select the card with the correct numeral, and hold it up when you say, "Show Me."

Variations:

- Hold up a flash card of a numeral. Have the children display the correct number of markers on their desks. Check for correct responses.

- Show-Me cards can also be used when practicing with flash cards. This way all students can participate.

How to Make Show-Me Cards
Materials:
   11 index cards per child
   black marker or crayon
   small plastic storage bag for each student

Give each child 11 cards and a small plastic storage bag. Have the children number their cards from 1 to 9, making a card for 0 and an extra 1. Store the Show-Me cards in the plastic bags for safe keeping.

Name: _____

Sorting and Graphing

Sort the bears by color. Write the number of each color on the line. Color in the graph to show how many bears.

red _____	yellow _____
orange _____	green _____

red										
yellow										
orange										
green										

At-Home Activities

Bears and Other Mammals

Bear Backpack

Literature: *I Love You with All My Heart*, by Noris Kern; *The Kissing Hand*, by Audrey Penn; *No Matter What*, by Debi Gliori

Materials: Backpack, copy of the book or books you want families to share (suggestions above), teddy bear, blank journal or notebook, small bag of candy hearts or chocolate drop-shaped candies, letter to parents (page 25), disposable camera (optional), heart stickers or other small rewards

Activity: Children will look forward to their chance to take home a class backpack. In a small backpack place one or more of the following books: *I Love You with All My Heart*, by Noris Kern; *The Kissing Hand*, by Audrey Penn; and/or *No Matter What*, by Debi Gliori. Add a teddy bear to the pack as well. Also put in the backpack a blank journal and a small bag of candy hearts or chocolate "drops." Finally, include a copy of the letter to parents. Parents should enjoy the special time they spend with their child reading the touching books about a mother's love. After reading the books, the parent and the child should record their thoughts in the journal that is provided. When the child returns the backpack to the class, ask him to share the journal entry and reward him with a heart sticker or a small bag of bear-shaped candies or cookies.

You might want to include a disposable camera in the backpack so pictures can be taken of families reading the books at home. When the film is developed, display the pictures in the classroom. Mothers might enjoy receiving copies of the pictures and the journal entries in cards for Mother's Day. (Please note that if a camera is not supplied in the backpack, the parent letter on page 25 will need to be revised to delete mention of the camera.)

Bears and Other Mammals

Animal Habitats Backpack

Literature: *In the Woods: Who's Been Here?* by Lindsay Barrett George; *The Family of Earth*, by Schim Schimmel

Materials: Backpack, plastic animal figures, habitat picture cards (four), parent letter (page 26), copy of *The Family of Earth,* blank journal, disposable camera (optional), stickers or other small reward

Activity: Read *In the Woods: Who's Been Here?* by Lindsay Barrett George, to your class. Discuss different kinds of animal homes in the woods and the animals that live there. (Examples: hollow tree—squirrel, underground burrow—chipmunk) Expand the discussion to include other places where animals live: in the jungle, on a farm, or underwater. Try to list some of the animals that live in these habitats and why they are suited to live there. Provide students with an opportunity to find examples of correct habitats for animals in other books.

As a follow-up activity, have students take turns bringing home a backpack that contains the book, *The Family of Earth*, by Schim Schimmel, which talks about how living things see the Earth differently depending on where they live. Include a bag of plastic animals and picture cards that reflect the habitats that you discussed. Children should work with their parents to sort the animals by habitat. They can do this step by placing each animal on the habitat that would provide the best home for it. Ask parents to work with their child or to check her work. You may want to write the names of the animals that should be included in each habitat on the back of the card for their convenience. A short entry can be added to the journal expressing thoughts about the activity.

Reward students when they return the backpack and share the journal entry. Stickers or a candy treat would do the trick!

(Please note that if the camera is not included in the backpack, the parent letter from page 26 will need to be revised.)

Bear Backpack

Dear Parents,

We have been very busy in class completing fun activities that relate to the topic of bears—real bears and imaginary bears with human qualities. I would like to include you in our studies by providing a few items for this special activity. To accomplish this goal, your child has brought home a special Bear Backpack. I have enclosed in this backpack a journal, a disposable camera, and books about the topic of a mother's love. This is how you can help:

1. Find some time to read at least one of the books with your child. You may do this in a number of ways: read the book to your child, have your child read the book, or take turns reading aloud every other page. (You are certainly welcome to read all three books!)

2. Assist your child in adding to the class journal. Together, write a short entry in the journal about any of the following topics: your favorite book, your favorite part of a book, or how you felt about this activity. You may:
   - write your child's thoughts.
   - take turns writing a short message.
   - let your child write his or her own response.
   - write the response and have your child draw a picture about the book.

3. Use the camera provided to have a picture taken of you and your child with a book from the backpack, reading together, or writing in the journal.

4. Repack the backpack and have your child return it to me. Please return the backpack by _____.

When all of the pictures on the camera have been taken, I will have them developed and display them in our classroom.

Thank you for participating in this activity. Your continued help and support are greatly appreciated.

Sincerely,

© Carson-Dellosa • CD-0584 Learning through Literature

Animal Habitats Backpack

Dear Parents,

We are learning about mammals and their habitats and would like to involve you in our classroom studies. To accomplish this goal and to provide your child with an opportunity to get a little more practice with this concept, I am sending home our classroom Animal Habitats Backpack. Inside you will find Schim Schimmel's book, *The Family of Earth*, a journal, four habitat cards, a bag of plastic animals, and a disposable camera. This is how you can help:

1. Read the book with your child. You may do this in a number of ways: read to your child, have your child read to you, or take turns reading aloud every other page.

2. Remove the habitat cards and plastic animals from the backpack and place them on a table. Identify and discuss each of the habitats. Have your child choose one of the animals, name it, and identify the habitat for which it is best suited by placing it on the correct habitat card.

3. Your child should be familiar with each of the habitats and the animals that live there since we have been studying this concept in class. We have read several books and practiced similar activities.

4. Feel free to discuss additional information about the animals by having your child share a fact, sharing a fact yourself, or each of you adding some new information about the topic.

5. Assist your child in contributing to the class journal. Together, write a short entry in the journal about any of the following topics: Share what you think about the book or the activity? Tell about something new that you learned from the book or during the activity. Describe your favorite animal or the habitat in which you would most like to live.

   You may:
   - take turns writing in the journal.
   - have your child write his or her thoughts.
   - act as the recorder by writing your child's response and encourage your child to draw a picture about the book or activity.

6. Use the camera provided to have a picture taken of you and your child reading together or writing in the journal.

7. Repack the backpack and have your child return it to me. Your child's efforts will be rewarded with a small treat. Please return the backpack by _____.

When all of the pictures on the camera have been taken, I will have them developed and display them in our classroom.

Thank you for participating in this activity.

                                                                                  Sincerely,

Dinosaurs

Young students love to learn about dinosaurs. In this section, we share a variety of fiction and nonfiction literature selections that capture students' interest in these prehistoric creatures. Learning is made fun and easy and dinosaurs come to life through movement, expression, shape books, and much more. This concept map will help you identify at a glance the kinds of activities we have provided to extend your study of dinosaurs across the curriculum.

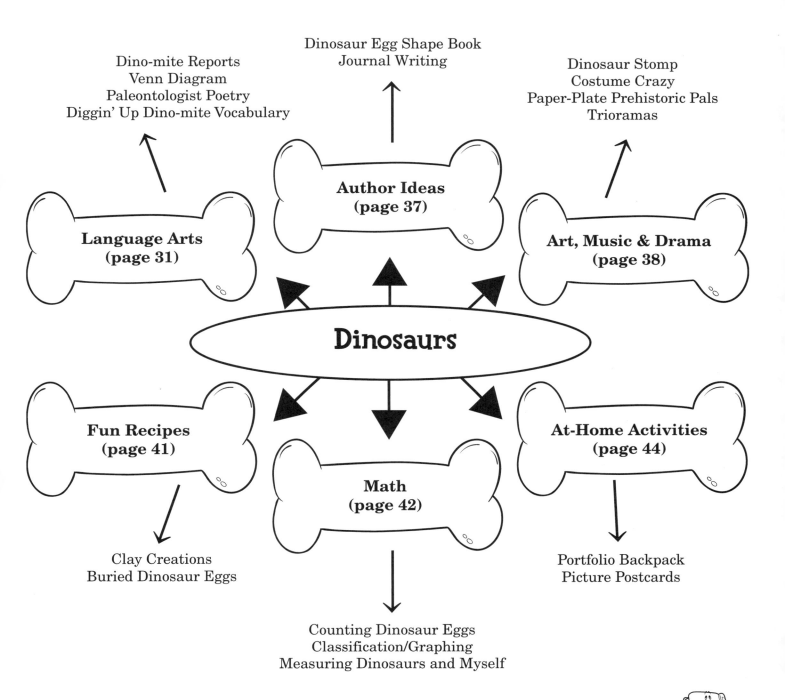

Literature Selections

Featured Literature

The following selections are used in conjunction with the activities in this section. You may want to obtain them from your library before you start the unit. (Activities with which the books are used are listed in parentheses.)

Nonfiction

Dinosaurs Laid Eggs, by Kate Petty (Copper Beech Books, 1997). Containing information about dinosaurs and other prehistoric reptiles, this picture book has so much information to share. Even the border on each page offers more facts for students to enjoy reading the second time around. This book also contains fun projects and true-or-false questions. (Classification/Graphing, page 42)

The Dinosaur Alphabet Book, by Jerry Pallotta (Charlesbridge Publishing, 1990). This alphabet book describes many dinosaur creatures of the past. (Dino-mite Reports, page 31)

Fiction

If the Dinosaurs Came Back, by Bernard Most (Harcourt Brace Jovanovich, 1978). This picture book introduces colorful dinosaurs to young readers. The story invites children to speculate on all of the fictional advantages they might enjoy if the dinosaurs came back. (Venn Diagram, page 31)

Saturday Night at the Dinosaur Stomp, by Carol Diggory Shields (Candlewick Press, 1997). Students will enjoy this story line in rhyme about the preparation and fun had by the dinosaurs at the Saturday Night Stomp! (Paleontologist Poetry, page 32; Dinosaur Stomp, page 38)

Little Grunt and the Big Egg: A Prehistoric Fairytale, by Tomie dePaola (Holiday House, 1990). Little Grunt brings home a very big egg. When a baby dinosaur is hatched, Little Grunt decides to keep the dinosaur for his pet. All babies grow up, however, and, boy, did Little Grunt's dinosaur grow! (Dinosaur Egg Shape Book, page 37)

Additional Suggested Literature

Nonfiction

Baby Dinosaurs, by "Dino" Don Lessem (Grosset & Dunlap, 2001). Within this wonderful book written by a true dinosaur enthusiast are pages filled with information, such as the dinosaurs' names, what the names mean, and facts about the dinosaurs (their size, their diet, and the time they lived). Each page presents a "Dino Don Says . . ." and most commonly asked questions are expressed in print and answered throughout. Marvelous illustrations accompany the "dino-mite" text.

© Carson-Dellosa • CD-0584 *Learning through Literature*

Dinosaurs

The Big Beast Book: Dinosaurs and How They Got That Way, by Jerry Booth (Little, Brown, 1988). This is a great teacher's aid when creating dinosaur projects and sharing facts.

Dinosaur Bones, by Bob Barner (Chronicle Books, 2001). The book shares with the reader how we can come to know the dinosaurs that lived many years ago by studying their bones. Illustrated with brilliant, colorful pictures, this book is written in rhyme and is useful as a teaching tool.

Dinosaur Valley, by Mitsuhiro Kurokawa (Chronicle Books, 1992). This fact-filled story is scientifically correct. The pictures alone are a valuable learning tool.

Dinosaurs, by Gail Gibbons (Holiday House, 1987). The author provides a simple but thorough introduction to dinosaurs and the basics of paleontology.

Dinosaurs (First Flaps, First Facts Series), by Teresa O'Brien (Flying Frog Publishing, 1998). Young children will enjoy this simple lift-the-flap introduction to familiar dinosaurs.

Dinosaurs Big and Small, by Kathleen Weidner Zoehfeld (HarperCollins Publishers, 2002). This wonderful story combines facts with modern day comparisons for a better understanding of the dinosaurs' height and weight.

Dinosaurs to Dodos: An Encyclopedia of Extinct Animals, by Don Lessem (Scholastic, Inc., 2000). This reference covers each of the prehistoric periods from the Precambrian Era to the Holocene Epoch (today). It may be too text-heavy for a read-aloud but provides good reference regarding the appearance of the animals, facts about them, and pronunciation of their names.

Gigantic: How Big Were the Dinosaurs? by Patrick O'Brien (Henry Holt and Company, 1999). Brief text and large illustrations show dinosaurs in comparison to familiar modern objects.

The Great Dinosaur Search, by Rosie Heywood (Usborne Publishing, Ltd., 2000). Provided in this fun seek-and-find book are brief facts about dinosaurs and other prehistoric creatures.

The Littlest Dinosaurs, by Bernard Most (Harcourt Brace Jovanovich, 1989). This book introduces the small dinosaurs, describing how big they actually were. The resource also provides interesting facts and its humorous approach will impress readers.

Marry Anning and the Sea Dragon, by Jeannine Atkins (Farrar Straus & Giroux, 1999). This is the true story of a young girl in nineteenth century England who discovers the skeleton of a prehistoric sea creature.

My Visit to the Dinosaurs, by Aliki (Crowell, 1985). This book is a great teaching tool, containing dinosaur vocabulary and facts.

More about Dinosaurs, by David Cutts (Troll Associates, 1982). An easy-to-read picture book, the text for each dinosaur introduced is one to two sentences in length throughout the 31-page book. The pages present simple facts and questions about what might have happened to the dinosaurs.

New Dinos, by Shelley Tanaka (Madison Press, 2003). This resource focuses on some of the most recent dinosaur discoveries.

World's Weirdest Dinosaurs, by M. L. Roberts (Whistlestop, 1996). Realistic pictures characterizing the strangest dinosaurs and the presentation of simple facts about each one make for an easy, informative read.

© Carson-Dellosa • CD-0584 *Learning through Literature*

Dinosaurs

Fiction

Danny and the Dinosaur, by Syd Hoff (Harper, 1958). Danny visits a museum and wonders what it would be like to play with a dinosaur. He meets a dinosaur who is wondering what it would be like to be outside playing. The two playmates share the day outside the museum learning new tricks. The dinosaur returns to the museum at the end of the day, after having the most enjoyable time he's had in a million years.

Dinosaur Bob and His Adventures with the Family Lazardo, by William Joyce (HarperCollins, 1995). What will the Lazardos bring back from their trip this time? While on a safari in Africa, they find Dinosaur Bob. Bob joins them on their trip to see many more interesting and real sites around the world, but will they be able to keep him?

Dinosaur Days, by Linda Manning (BridgeWater Books, 1994). Featuring a week's worth of seven silly dinosaur visitors, this book reinforces numbers and days of the week.

Dinosaurs Forever, by William Wise (Dial Books for Young Readers, 2000). Here's a collection of 21 fabulous dinosaur poems.

The Magic School Bus in the Time of the Dinosaurs, by Joanna Cole and Bruce Degen (Scholastic, Inc., 1994). The popular Magic School Bus gang travels in the magic bus back in time to prehistory.

Tyrannosaurus Was a Beast, by Jack Prelutsky (Greenwillow Books, 1988). This collection of catchy poems about dinosaurs will entertain young learners.

Whatever Happened to the Dinosaurs? by Bernard Most (Harcourt Brace Jovanovich, 1984). The author explores some amusing possibilities explaining the disappearance of the dinosaurs.

Language Arts

Dinosaurs

Dino-mite Reports

Literature: *The Dinosaur Alphabet Book*, by Jerry Pallotta

Materials: Reproducibles (pages 33 and 34), large brown grocery bags, scissors, pencils, waterproof markers, paint and brushes

Activity: After reading *The Dinosaur Alphabet Book*, by Jerry Pallotta, ask students to select one of the dinosaurs they are interested in researching. Using an informational program on the classroom computer or other nonfiction literature selections, have students research and record new information about their dinosaurs of choice. Students may complete the "Tracking Down the Facts" Report Form (page 33) or they can write in paragraph form using the open sheet on page 34.

Dinosaur replicas can be made by drawing the animals on large brown grocery bags. Ask students to bring in grocery bags from home until enough are available for each child to have one. Cut each bag so that it can be opened to lie flat. Have each student draw a large outline of the dinosaur she has researched and then paint it. The paint and details look best when the pencil outline is redrawn with waterproof marker after the painting is dry. Staple the report to the back of the painting. Once the information is gathered and the paper bag dinosaurs are complete, the reports can be presented to others around your school. As students hold up the flattened grocery bags to read their reports, the audience will be looking at the painted dinosaur pictures.

Venn Diagram

Literature: *If the Dinosaurs Came Back*, by Bernard Most

Materials: Venn diagram (page 35), small photograph of each student, small dinosaur pictures or stickers, pencils

Activity: Read *If the Dinosaurs Came Back*, by Bernard Most, to the class. Then engage the students in a discussion about what it would be like to live with these now extinct creatures. You can practice the important skill of comparing and contrasting using a Venn diagram to show how humans differ from dinosaurs. Prepare for each student a copy of page 35 by placing a sticker or picture of a dinosaur in the specified square and a photo of the child in the other square. As a class, brainstorm some ways in which we are like and different from dinosaurs and then demonstrate how to use a Venn diagram to indicate these similarities and differences. Students should enjoy using their own photos to practice this important skill!

Dinosaurs

Paleontologist Poetry

Literature: *Saturday Night at the Dinosaur Stomp*, by Carol Diggory Shields

Activity: Students will enjoy the book, *Saturday Night at the Dinosaur Stomp*, by Carol Diggory Shields. Shields uses rhyme to describe the fun dinosaurs have at the Saturday Night Stomp. Discuss that the story is written in rhyme and invite your students to identify the words that sound alike. It is important to point out that although the story is written in rhyme, it also has a story line. Reinforce the use of rhyme through a choral reading of the book. You could also chart a portion of this book or another dinosaur poem and cover the rhyming words. Allow students to replace those words with their own vocabulary words. Model this type of poetry by writing a class poem together. Then invite your students to create their own poems independently or in small groups. Remember to use parent volunteers! As students dictate their poetry, volunteers can write or type the poems to conserve time.

Diggin' Up Dino-mite Vocabulary

Materials: Reproducible (page 36), plastic storage bags, pencils, scissors

Activity: Help students to become familiar with the vocabulary they need to know by using the reproducible on page 36. These word cards can be used as the words come up during class instruction and shared reading time or introduced as words for the day. Children should place their vocabulary words in a plastic storage bag for safekeeping. They can practice reading the words both in class and at home. You may also choose to display enlarged copies of the words in the classroom to enable students to become more familiar with them. Record any new words on the blank bones for students to learn.

"Tracking Down the Facts" Report Form

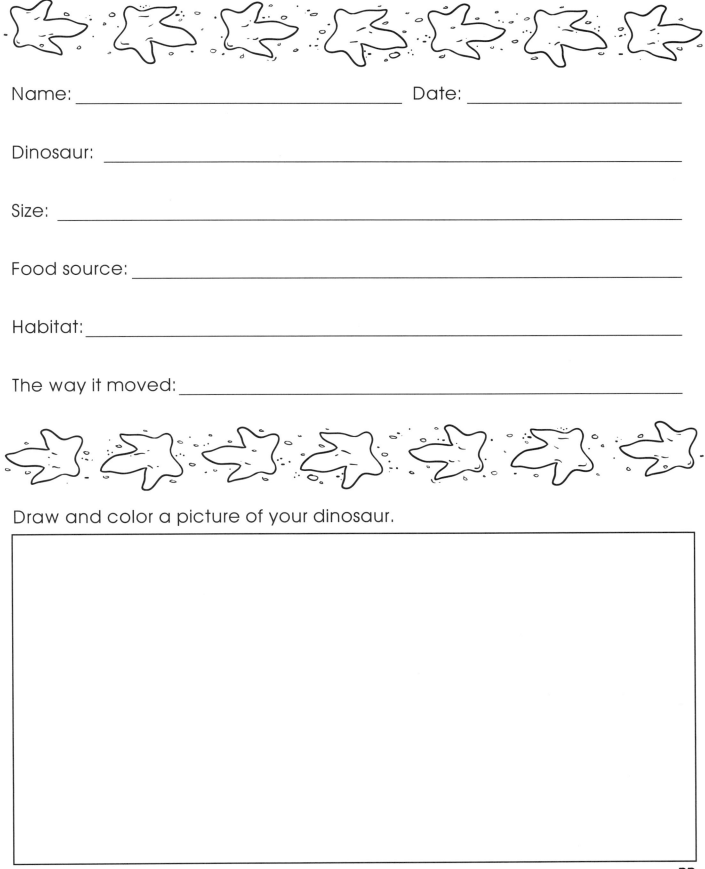

Name: _____ Date: _____

Dinosaur: _____

Size: _____

Food source: _____

Habitat: _____

The way it moved: _____

Draw and color a picture of your dinosaur.

© Carson-Dellosa • CD-0584 *Learning through Literature*

Report Form

Name: _____

Date: _____

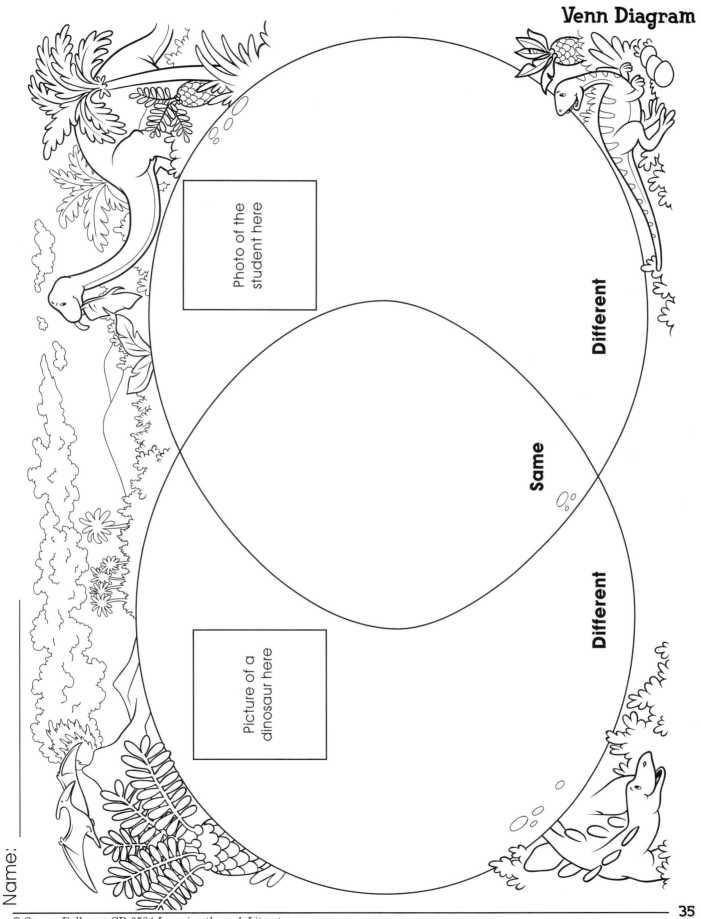

Diggin' Up Dino-mite Vocabulary

Use these cards to learn new words as we study dinosaurs. Cut them apart and store them in a plastic bag so that you do not lose them. Fill in words of your own on the blank bones.

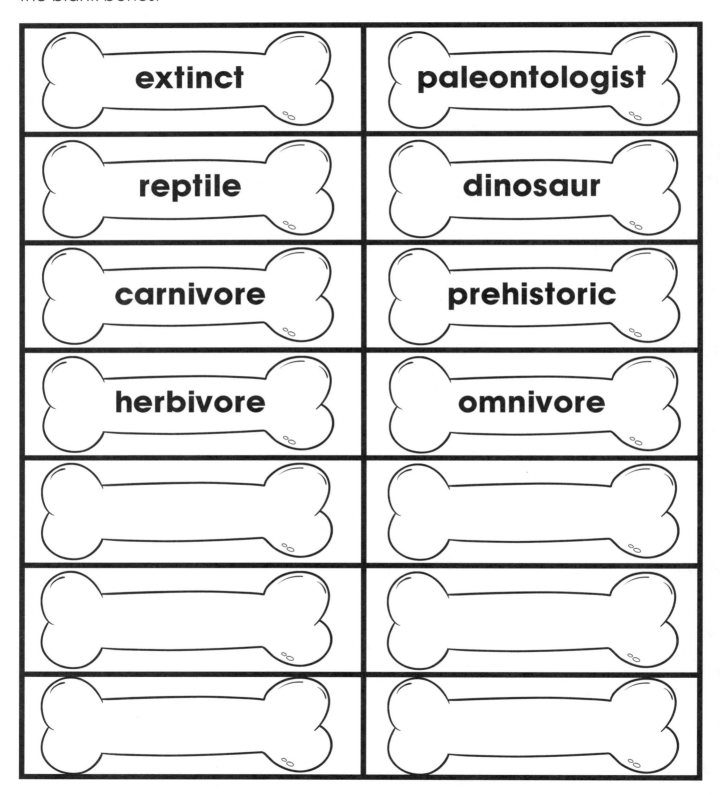

Author Ideas

Dinosaurs

Dinosaur Egg Shape Book

Literature: *Little Grunt and the Big Egg: A Prehistoric Fairytale,* by Tomie dePaola

Materials: Heavy construction paper, scissors, white notebook paper, stapler, pencils, photograph of each student (optional)

Activity: Tomie dePaola provides a perfect springboard for young authors in his story, *Little Grunt and the Big Egg.* Just as Little Grunt wants to keep his hatched dinosaur as a pet, have students imagine what it would be like to have a pet dinosaur that laid 10 eggs. They can create their stories in egg-shaped booklets. For each book, cut two pieces of heavy construction paper into the shape of large eggs to be used for the front and back covers. Then cut several egg-shaped pieces of white notebook paper and staple these sheets between the covers to create a book for each child. (Parents or older students could perform this time-consuming task for you.) Each student can write his story on the notebook pages, illustrate the front cover, and add a photo to the author page. Younger students can dictate their stories to volunteers. Be sure to allow time for your authors to share their "egg-citing" stories!

Journal Writing

Materials: Student journals, pencils

Activity: It is important to provide your students with ample opportunities to write. Regular practice enables them to express their creative ideas and hone their writing skills. Daily journal writing can provide this opportunity. The following story starters may be helpful to your students, but you will certainly be able to add your own based on various books that support classroom instruction.

- A dinosaur came to school today. I could tell because . . .
- I have a pet dinosaur named . . .
- I hid my dinosaur in my bedroom until . . .
- Dinosaurs used to be extinct but I saw one today at the . . .
- I'm like the Tyrannosaurus Rex because we both . . .
- I'm different from the Tyrannosaurus Rex because . . .

You may want to provide fill-in-the-blank story skeletons for younger students. One example of a fill-in-the-blank story follows:

My dinosaur's name is _____. He is a _____. He has _____ legs and is the color _____. One thing many people don't know about him is _____.

Art, Music & Drama

Dinosaur Stomp

Literature: *Saturday Night at the Dinosaur Stomp*, by Carol Diggory Shields

Materials: Pictures of various dinosaurs (from books or magazines)

Activity: Wouldn't it be fun to move and stomp about the room or on the playground like a dinosaur? Name a dinosaur and hold up its picture. Ask the students to move about the room the way they think that dinosaur did. This can be a silent activity displaying movement only, or students can growl, caw, or grunt some dinosaur sounds. Carol Diggory Shields' book, *Saturday Night at the Dinosaur Stomp*, is a great book to use with this activity.

Costume Crazy

Materials: Buttons, construction paper, crayons and/or markers, large brown grocery bags, scissors, glue, other decorative materials, plastic eggs, "artifacts" (facts written on paper, candy treats)

Activity: Students may enjoy creating paleontologist vests out of large brown grocery bags. Here's how:

1. Cut the "front" of the bag straight up the center, and then cut a hole for the child's neck. Fold down the "collar" flaps or cut them off.

2. Cut one armhole on each side of the bag.

3. Trim the bottom of the bag to resemble a vest.

4. Students can decorate their vests with crayons, markers, real buttons, and paper pockets.

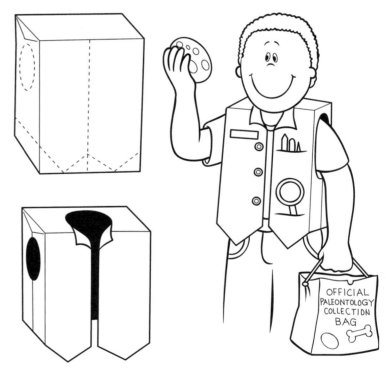

Wouldn't it be fun to go on an exploration looking for artifacts? Obtain plastic eggs (sold inexpensively in the spring) and place in each egg an interesting fact about dinosaurs, a candy treat, or another surprise. Then, hide the eggs around the classroom or on the school grounds. Students—wearing their completed vests and armed with collection bags—can search for the dinosaur eggs and place them carefully inside their bags. Be creative and let your students have fun exploring.

Dinosaurs

Paper-Plate Prehistoric Pals

Materials: Large paper plates, scissors, markers and/or crayons, craft sticks, glue, paint and brushes

Activity: It is recommended that you or another adult cut out holes for the eyes and give each paper plate a "shape" prior to distributing the plates (to avoid injury to students while cutting and poking holes). Give each student one large paper plate. Children will enjoy adding bright colors, spots, teeth, and other details to create dinosaur faces. When they finish, glue a craft stick to the bottom of each plate to make an easy-to-hold handle for each mask. Now students can parade throughout the school or visit other classrooms stomping, growling, and even looking like real dinosaurs!

It is fun to ask students to place their masks at chin level and take a picture. The photos of a smiling face with each mask can be displayed or mailed home as postcards.

Trioramas

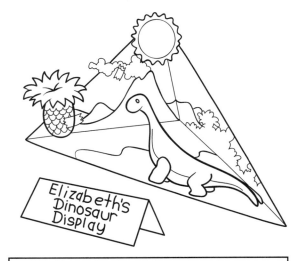

Materials: Construction paper, scissors, glue, markers, crayons, directions for the triorama (page 40)

Activity: Students may enjoy learning more about dinosaurs by identifying elements of their habitats. Allow them to be very creative by constructing trioramas.

Here are some items and information you may wish to encourage each child to include:

- habitat (Where did the dinosaurs live?)
- food (What did they eat? Plants, smaller dinosaurs, eggs, etc.)
- water supply
- plant life
- dinosaur(s)

Once you have determined what information you will want your students to demonstrate that they have learned, share your goals with them. You may do a class example together, talking through the options students will have. If you will be taking a grade on this project, create a point checklist so students know exactly on what elements they will be graded and the point value of each. See the example at right.

Dino-mite Work! Triorama Grade

habitat (5 points)	5
food (5 points)	3
water (5 points)	5
plants (5 points)	3
dinosaur (10 points)	10
Total	26/30 Great

© Carson-Dellosa • CD-0584 *Learning through Literature*

Making the Habitat (A Triorama)

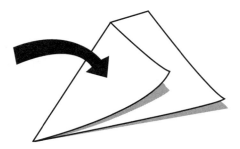

1. Fold a sheet of construction paper from one corner down to the bottom of the opposite side. Cut off the excess to make a square construction paper sheet. Save the excess paper.

2. Fold the two opposite corners together so that you have made a triangle. When you unfold the paper, you should have a square with two creases that cross in the center.

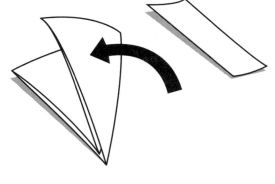

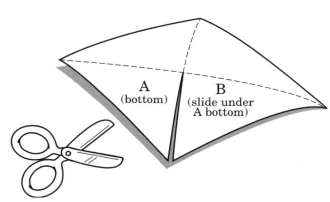

3. Cut from one of the corners up the crease to the center. Then slide one cut edge over the other to meet at the next crease and make a triangular base. Glue the flaps to secure the base. You now have a triorama in which a student can display a dinosaur and its habitat.

4. Students can add background details with crayons or markers or use both techniques to add variety and textures. Plant life, the sun, water, and perhaps even a volcano can be added using construction paper, scissors, and glue. Make these pieces separately and position them to give the triorama a three-dimensional look. Take the excess paper you set aside in step 1 and fold it in half the long way. This may be placed in front of the finished triorama to display the title, the student's name, and information about the dinosaur.

© Carson-Dellosa • CD-0584 *Learning through Literature*

Fun Recipes

Clay Creations

Materials: Wooden spoon, large pan, stove or electric burner, 2 c. (474 mL) flour, $1/2$ c. (119 mL) cornstarch, 1 tbsp. (15 mL) powdered alum, 1 c. (237 mL) salt, 1 tbsp. (15 mL) salad oil, 2 c. (480 mL) water, food coloring (optional), foil or waxed paper (optional), toothpicks (optional)

Activity: Students will enjoy reading and learning about dinosaurs, but creating a dinosaur will allow your students the opportunity to demonstrate what they understand. This is a great tactile activity for those students who need to get involved physically in the learning process!

Mix the flour, cornstarch, alum, salt, oil, and water in the pan. To make a batch of clay that is only one color, add food coloring to the mixture at this point. Otherwise, divide the dough into batches and add a different color to each batch. Stir constantly over low heat until the mixture thickens into a doughlike consistency. Remove it from the heat and let the clay cool. Once it is cool enough to be handled, place the clay on foil, waxed paper, or a countertop and knead until smooth. For a class of 25 students, you may want to mix four batches of clay. Add a different color of food coloring to each batch to create dinosaurs with a variety of colors.

Students will have lots of fun molding their dinosaurs and creating miniature characters. Challenge some of your more advanced students by providing them with toothpicks to put inside their dinosaurs' bodies to strengthen the necks and support the legs.

Once the clay creations are completed, have students set them inside their triorama habitats (see pages 39 and 40) to dry overnight. (The clay will harden if left out in the open air. It will stay pliable and moist if stored in an airtight container.) After the clay has hardened, students can add finishing touches by painting details such as spots and eyes on their dinosaurs.

Buried Dinosaur Eggs

Materials: Chocolate pudding (spoon into foam cups or use individual pudding cups), plastic spoons, jelly beans (spotted "eggs" look best), plenty of napkins

Activities: While it is fun to read and learn, students may also become motivated by eating "buried dinosaur eggs." This easy combination of sweet treats will allow students to dig into their "work" just like the paleontologists do.

Give each student her own pudding portion and five or six jelly beans. (Make sure none of your students has food allergies before using the snack idea. For students with an allergy to chocolate, you can provide butterscotch pudding.) Give students spoons and napkins and have them "bury" their dinosaur eggs in the pudding. Then invite them to dig in and enjoy their prehistoric finds!

© Carson-Dellosa • CD-0584 *Learning through Literature*

Math

Counting Dinosaur Eggs

Materials: Heavy construction paper, water-based marker, scissors

Activity: Students will enjoy using dinosaur eggs to practice their numbers. Draw 10 or more egg shapes on heavy construction paper. Program the bottom of each egg with a certain number of dots. Label the top half with the corresponding numeral. Cut out the eggs. Then, as you cut them apart make this activity self checking by cutting each egg with a different-shaped line. Laminate the pieces for durability. Place these egg puzzles at a math center for the students to put together.

You may modify this learning station for older students by concentrating on place value. Use the standard form of a large number on the top half of the egg and the expanded form of the same number on the bottom. Eggs-cellent work!

Classification/Graphing

Literature: *Dinosaurs Laid Eggs*, by Kate Petty

Materials: Jelly beans, foil-covered chocolate eggs, or plastic eggs; paper; crayons

Activity: After reading *Dinosaurs Laid Eggs*, by Kate Petty, distribute jelly beans, foil-covered chocolate eggs, or plastic eggs to the students. Have them sort the eggs according to color and draw tally marks to record their results on paper. As a class, create a pictograph to show the combined results. Alternatively, have students vote for their favorite color egg and graph those results.

Measuring Dinosaurs and Myself

Materials: Reproducible (page 43), bathroom scale, tape measure, pencils

Activity: Give each student a copy of the reproducible from page 43. Encourage students to weigh themselves and measure their heights, recording their measurements on their sheets. Next, have them read the measurements of the dinosaurs described on the reproducible. Students should circle the correct answers in the sentences and place their names along with the dinosaur names in order from largest to smallest in size. Remind the children that they are comparing only their measurements with the dinosaurs listed on the paper.

Measuring Dinosaurs and Myself

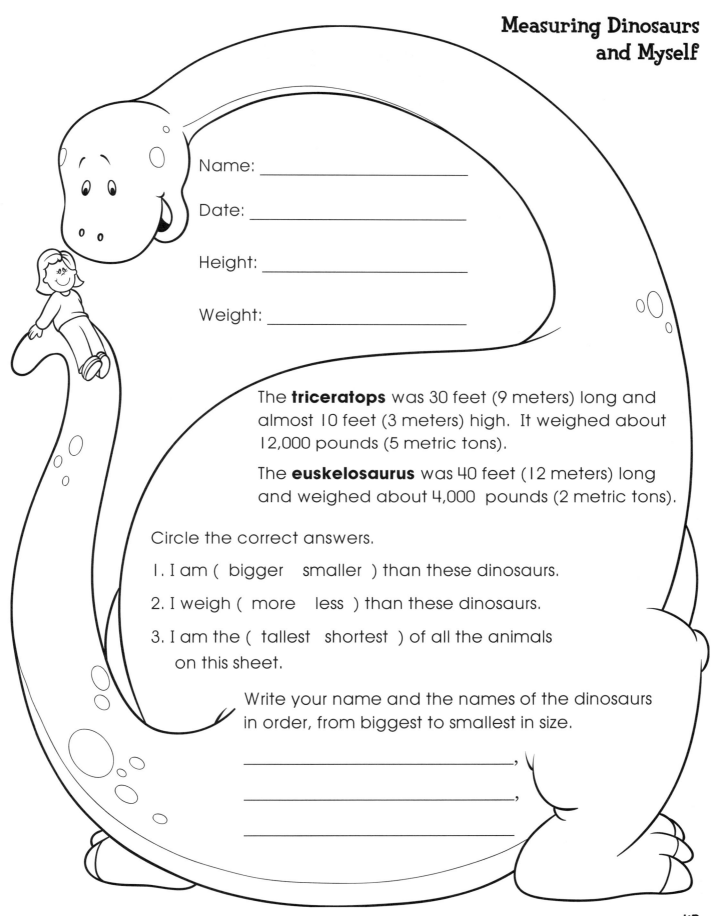

Name: _____

Date: _____

Height: _____

Weight: _____

The **triceratops** was 30 feet (9 meters) long and almost 10 feet (3 meters) high. It weighed about 12,000 pounds (5 metric tons).

The **euskelosaurus** was 40 feet (12 meters) long and weighed about 4,000 pounds (2 metric tons).

Circle the correct answers.

1. I am (bigger   smaller) than these dinosaurs.

2. I weigh (more   less) than these dinosaurs.

3. I am the (tallest   shortest) of all the animals on this sheet.

Write your name and the names of the dinosaurs in order, from biggest to smallest in size.

_____,

_____,

_____

At-Home Activities

Portfolio Backpack

Materials: Backpack, portfolio (construction paper or manila folder), crayons or markers, student dinosaur projects from this unit, reproducibles (pages 45 and 46), vocabulary cards (optional), dinosaur puzzle or model (optional), videotape and video camera (optional)

Activity: A take-home portfolio can be as simple as a sheet of construction paper folded in half, or as formal as an expandable legal-sized manila folder. Pass out the folder of your choice and provide your students time to decorate and personalize their folders. One way to do this is to allow the children to work while you are reading a new dinosaur book aloud.

The portfolio can be sent home in a backpack at the end of the unit. Place all of the projects the student has completed in the portfolio: the research report, mask, shape book, paleontologist vest, and journal. Be sure these entries are dated so you can document the student's progress and understanding throughout the year. Include copies of the Parent Letter from page 45 and the Creature Critic from page 46. You may wish to write a personalized note on the Creature Critic sheet.

The backpack can also contain manipulatives with which to review skills. Vocabulary word cards, stored in a plastic bag, can be reinforced at home. Families can also work together on dinosaur puzzles or models.

Families can get an inside peek at your class's activities with a classroom video. Capture on tape all the fun and exciting moments of your unit, like the young paleontologists wearing their vests on an egg hunt, constructing masks, and stomping like dinosaurs. Professional quality is not expected. The smiles and learning reflected in the video will say it all!

Before the backpack is returned to school, parents can supply feedback by completing the Creature Critic sheet that you have included. This invites parents to communicate their thoughts regarding their child's progress or classroom projects. Alternatively, students can also complete the form.

Picture Postcards

Materials: Photographs of students with dinosaur projects, class addresses, postcard stamps

Activity: Make parents a part of the learning experience by sending picture postcards to their homes. Take a photo of each student holding his mask or shape book, wearing his vest, or standing by his triorama. Develop the pictures. Have students write short messages to their parents on the backs of the pictures. Computer-generated address labels would make addressing the cards easy. Have children bring in money for stamps, or your parent-teacher organization may be willing to contribute to your postage fund. Mail the postcards to your students' homes. Parents are sure to treasure this keepsake!

© Carson-Dellosa • CD-0584 *Learning through Literature*

Portfolio Backpack

Dear Parent,

We have been having a "dino-mite" time learning about the dinosaurs. The contents of this portfolio will allow you to see your child's progress throughout the unit, give feedback, and ask questions. Please take some time to review your child's work, or better yet, have your child explain each project to you. Please fill out the Creature Critic form and return it along with the backpack and all of its contents by _____.

After you and your child have reflected on the projects, you can review the enclosed vocabulary words and put the dinosaur puzzle together. We hope this backpack effectively communicates some of the things we have been doing here at school and allows you and your child to have a dino-mite time together! Thank you for your continued support.

Sincerely,

Creature Critic

Name: _____

I like _____
_____
_____
_____

An idea or
thought I have is _____
_____
_____
_____

A question I have is _____
_____
_____
_____

Frogs and Other Amphibians

Kids love learning about animals. Even very young children have a great deal of knowledge on this topic from experiences with animals at the zoo as well as pets and other common animals they may encounter in their neighborhoods. Opportunities for curriculum integration are varied and many, as you can see with this concept map.

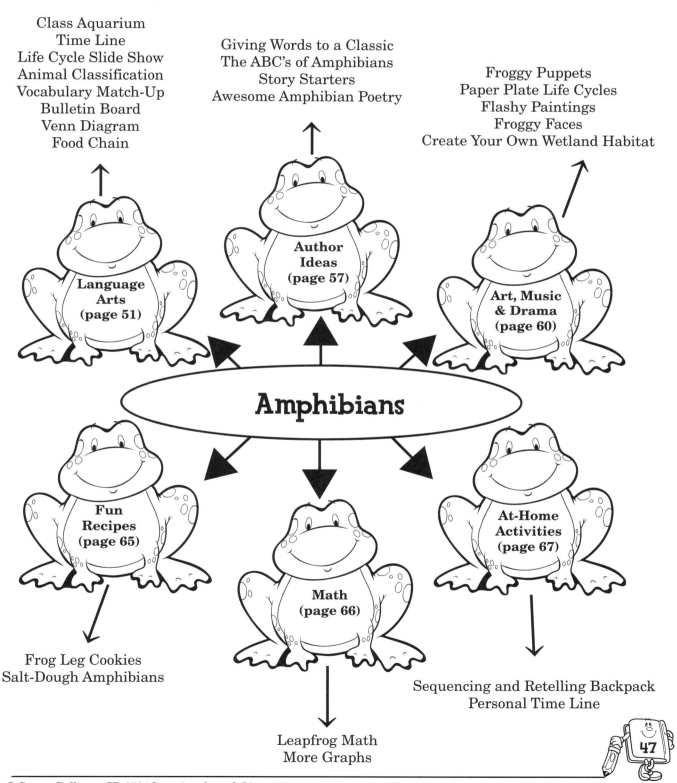

Class Aquarium
Time Line
Life Cycle Slide Show
Animal Classification
Vocabulary Match-Up
Bulletin Board
Venn Diagram
Food Chain

Giving Words to a Classic
The ABC's of Amphibians
Story Starters
Awesome Amphibian Poetry

Froggy Puppets
Paper Plate Life Cycles
Flashy Paintings
Froggy Faces
Create Your Own Wetland Habitat

Language Arts (page 51)

Author Ideas (page 57)

Art, Music & Drama (page 60)

Amphibians

Fun Recipes (page 65)

Math (page 66)

At-Home Activities (page 67)

Frog Leg Cookies
Salt-Dough Amphibians

Leapfrog Math
More Graphs

Sequencing and Retelling Backpack
Personal Time Line

© Carson-Dellosa • CD-0584 *Learning through Literature*

Literature Selections

Featured Literature

The following selections are used in conjunction with the activities in this section. You may want to obtain them from your library before you start the unit. (Activities with which the books are used are listed in parentheses.)

Nonfiction

About Amphibians: A Guide for Children, by Cathryn Sill (Peachtree, 2000). Brief descriptions and realistic illustrations explain the basic characteristics of amphibians. (Venn Diagram, page 53)

Amphibian, by Barry Clarke (Knopf, 1993). This is an excellent resource for both teacher and student. The amount of text may make it unsuitable as a read-aloud for young children, but it is a good reference with fascinating photographs. (Food Chain, page 54)

Amphibians, by Melissa Stewart (Children's Press, 2001). This book provides good definitions and examples of frogs, toads, and salamanders. Also included is a section on the role amphibians play in our lives. (Animal Classification, page 52)

Australian Frogs, by Carolyn MacLulich (Sidney Scholastic, 1996). This simple text is a brief overview of frogs with color photographs. It is suitable for a beginning reader. (The ABC's of Amphibians, page 57)

Fantastic Frogs, by Fay Robinson (Scholastic, 1999). Using simple sentence structure and repetitive language, this book provides great background information about the appearance, habitat, and life cycle of different frogs. (The ABC's of Amphibians, page 57)

Flashy, Fantastic Rain Forest Frogs, by Dorothy Hinshaw Patent (Walker and Co., 1997). A great resource about the different types of frogs that live in the rain forest, this book's bright, colorful illustrations make it an exciting read. (Flashy Paintings, page 61)

The Frog, by Sally Tagholm (Kingfisher, 2000). The life of the frog is examined from birth to breeding and in its daily life. The story-like format of the text makes this nonfiction more friendly to young readers. (Life Cycle Slide Show, page 52)

Salamanders, by Edward Maruska (Child's World, 1997). A perfect introduction to this amphibian, this book's easy-to-understand format describes the salamander's defenses, babies, location, and more. (The ABC's of Amphibians, page 57)

Tale of a Tadpole, by Karen Wallace (DK Publishing Inc., 1988). This easy-to-read nonfiction book uses simple vocabulary and stunning photography to explain the life cycle of a frog. (Time Line, page 51; Paper Plate Life Cycles, page 60)

Frogs and Other Amphibians

Fiction

A Boy, a Dog, and a Frog, by Mercer Mayer (Dial Press, 1967). In this classic wordless book, a frog continues to outwit a small boy who is trying to catch him, but when the boy and his dog head home, the frog is lonely and follows them. (Giving Words to a Classic, page 57)

Bugs for Lunch, by Margery Facklam (Charlesbridge, 1999). The rhyming text presents many animals, including toads, that feast on insects. (Food Chain, page 54)

Frog Goes to Dinner, by Mercer Mayer (Dial Press, 1974). The lovable boy and his rascally pet frog are back for another wordless adventure. This time the two friends wreak havoc at a fancy restaurant. (Giving Words to a Classic, page 57)

Gilbert de la Frogponde: A Swamp Story, by Jennifer Rae (Peachtree Publishers, 1997). A fat, lazy frog must convince two chefs that frog legs are not as tasty as they believe. Instead, Gilbert tries to persuade them that insects are all the rave! (Frog Leg Cookies, page 65)

Growing Frogs, by Vivian French (Candlewick Press, 2000). A little girl collects frog spawn at a local pond and the reader follows the growth stages. This picture book is written with the story at the top of each page and factual information at the bottom of each page. There is also an index, which makes this lively story a good first reference. (Class Aquarium, page 51)

In the Small, Small Pond, by Denise Fleming (Henry Holt, 1993). Written in rhyme, this easy-to-read picture book is filled with beautiful illustrations that capture the pond, an active frog, and the changing seasons. (Create Your Own Wetlands Habitat, page 62)

Jump, Frog, Jump! by Robert Kalan (Greenwillow Books, 1981). This cumulative tale describes a wetlands food chain. A frog in the food chain faces danger from turtles and snakes and his only escape is to jump, frog, jump! (Sequencing and Retelling Backpack, page 67)

Let's Go, Froggy! by Jonathan London (Viking, 1994). First in a series about a young frog who has all kinds of adventures. (Froggy Puppets, page 60)

The Mysterious Tadpole, by Steven Kellogg (Dial Press, 1977). Louis receives what everyone believes to be a tadpole for his birthday. The tadpole grows into a very large and very unusual "frog" and has several adventures in the school swimming pool. (Story Starters, page 58)

The Salamander Room, by Anne Mazer (Knopf, 1991). A boy wants to keep a salamander as a pet and ends up creating a forest habitat in his bedroom. The story provides an interesting introduction to animal habitats. (Create Your Own Wetlands Habitat, page 62)

Tuesday, by David Wiesner (Clarion Books, 1991). Frogs overtake a quiet community and in the morning limp lily pads are all that's left behind. This nearly wordless book provides many opportunities for students to create their own text. The book is a winner of the Caldecott Medal. (Story Starters, page 58)

Frogs and Other Amphibians

Additional Suggested Literature

Nonfiction

The Frog Alphabet Book, by Jerry Pallotta (Charlesbridge, 1990). Different types of frogs and other amphibians from A to Z with realistic illustrations are featured in this book.

Frogs, by Gail Gibbons (Holiday House, 1993). In this very thorough introduction to frogs, young readers will learn about the life cycle, habitat, lifestyle, body parts, and enemies of frogs through text and labeled illustrations.

How Do Frogs Swallow with Their Eyes? Questions and Answers about Amphibians, by Melvin and Gilda Berger (Scholastic Inc., 2002). Question-and-answer is the format for this nonfiction book about frogs, toads, salamanders, and newts. Although not necessarily a book to be read aloud cover-to-cover with students, the colorful illustrations and straightforward answers will hold a their attention through several pertinent questions.

Fiction

The Adventures of Frog and Toad, by Arnold Lobel (HarperCollins, 1998). This book includes the classics *Frog and Toad Are Friends*, *Days with Frog and Toad*, and *Frog and Toad Together*. These timeless stories of friendship and adventure are not to be missed by any youngster!

Bently & Egg, by William Joyce (HarperCollins, 1992). Bently is a frog who is entrusted to watch over his best friend's egg. The adventure begins when the egg is kidnapped.

The Frog Principal, by Stephanie Calmenson (Scholastic Press, 2001). A school's favorite principal is accidentally turned into a frog by a blundering magician.

It's a Frog's Life! by Steve Parker (Reader's Digest Children's Pub., 1999). This book is actually a diary written from a unique perspective—a frog's. Complete with captioned illustrations, newspaper clippings, a glossary, and pond samples, this frog's scrapbook is one worth poring over.

It's Mine, by Leo Lionni (Knopf, 1986). Three frogs begin to get greedy and possessive until they are rescued by a large toad. This book provides a wonderful springboard for discussing the topics of sharing and friendship.

Philippe in Monet's Garden, by Lisa Jobe Carmack (Museum of Fine Arts, Boston, 1999). Running away from the frog catchers who want his tasty frog legs, Philippe finds a happy home in the Paris countryside. He enters Claude Monet's garden, where no frog hunting is allowed. A brief biographical sketch of Monet is included as well as a reproduction of his painting, *Water Lilies*.

Language Arts

Frogs and Other **Amphibians**

Class Aquarium

Literature: *Growing Frogs,* by Vivian French

Materials: Clear aquarium tank, sea rocks, plastic water plants, distilled water, tadpoles, science journals, magnifying glasses, fish food, equipment to oxygenate the water (available at pet stores)

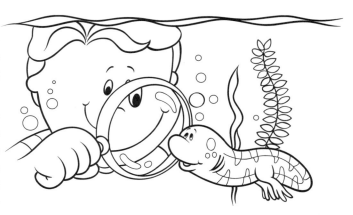

Activity: Set the stage for your unit on amphibians by preparing a class aquarium. Fill a large clear tank with sea rocks, plastic water plants available at pet stores, and distilled water. Set up the equipment to add oxygen to the water for the tadpole stage. The day the unit is to begin, add several tadpoles to your aquarium. As you introduce the tadpoles into your classroom, read aloud *Growing Frogs* by Vivian French. In it, a little girl decides to collect frog spawn and watch it develop into tadpoles and then frogs in her aquarium. Children will love the similarities between the main character and their class as both prepare to "grow frogs." Allow students to name the new class pets. Keep a basket full of science journals, magnifying glasses, and fish food on the shelf beside the aquarium. Provide plenty of time for students to observe the tadpoles. As the unit progresses and students learn more about a frog's stages of growth, have them document their observations of the tadpoles in each of those stages. Pictures and words can be recorded in the science journals.

As the tadpoles reach maturation, be sure to drain most of the water from the tank and add large rocks so the frogs can breathe air. Encourage students to continue taking notes on the amphibians in their journals. Young scientists can watch their sleeping patterns, eating habits, playfulness, and general activity. Allow time for students to share their observations orally.

Time Line

Literature: *Tale of a Tadpole*, by Karen Wallace

Materials: Time line sheet for each student, pencils and crayons

Activity: A perfect addition to the beginning of your unit is *Tale of a Tadpole,* by Karen Wallace. The uncomplicated vocabulary and striking photos in this nonfiction book provide the perfect inspiration for this project. Students can create a time line of a frog's development based on this book (or later, in the unit, on the growth actually observed). Begin by drawing a large time line across the chalkboard. Give each student a copy of a blank time line to complete as you model yours. Discuss each stage of growth beginning with eggs. Write "egg" at the beginning of your time line. Illustrate and briefly describe the stage. Continue the lesson to include tadpole, growing back legs, and finally, a full-grown frog. Help the students to write a brief summary of their observations at each stage of development.

Frogs and Other Amphibians

Life Cycle Slide Show

Literature: *The Frog*, by Sally Tagholm

Materials: Digital camera; paper, crayons, markers, and a computer scanner; or computer painting software

Activity: Examine the stages of growth with *The Frog*, by Sally Tagholm. Young learners will find the narrative format of this nonfiction book very familiar and easy to follow. Students can apply what they learned by creating slide shows showing the life cycle of frogs. Break the class into cooperative groups of four. Each group will design a series of four slides depicting each stage of the life cycle, one slide for each growth stage.

You have the option of instructing your students to create slides in several ways: digital photos taken of a classroom observation tank, student-made illustrations that will be scanned, or pictures created in a computer software program. The level of students' computer proficiency and the number of volunteers you can get will help you reach this decision. Regardless of how they originate, each slide will end up in the computer. Cooperative groups will then work to sequence their slides and add narration to explain the changes occurring throughout the stages of growth. Remember to have each group add a title slide and an author's slide. Plan plenty of time for your class to view all of the programs. Bring popcorn because the finished products will be a show to remember!

Animal Classification

Literature: *Amphibians*, by Melissa Stewart

Materials: Old magazine pictures of animals, construction paper, scissors, glue, chart paper, tape

Activity: After introducing the term "amphibian" to your class, read *Amphibians*, by Melissa Stewart, to strengthen your students' comprehension. Frogs, toads, and salamanders are all well defined in this resource. Students will then have fun categorizing for review. Cut out pictures of all types of animals, including reptiles, bird, mammals, and, of course, amphibians. Mount the pictures on colorful construction paper and laminate them for durability. Label two charts "amphibians" and "not amphibians." Pass out the animal pictures. One at a time, invite children to approach the two charts, tape the picture to the correct chart, and explain *why* it belongs there.

Variation: If your students are learning to classify all types of animals, create more charts and label them accordingly.

Frogs and Other Amphibians

Vocabulary Match-Up

Materials: Paper frog and lily pad patterns (reproducible, page 55), water-based marker, tape

Activity: Practice vocabulary terms with this matching game. Program frog cutouts with words from your unit of study and write the matching definitions on the lily pads. Arrange the lily pads on a pond drawn on chart paper. Have students place each frog on its corresponding lily pad.

Variation: This game can be used in other subject areas as well. Write math facts and answers on the frogs and lily pads or use the cutouts to practice antonyms and synonyms in reading class. You can reuse the frog and lily pad cutouts if you laminate them before you write on them. Use a water-based marker to write the words or numerals the students will practice. When they have completed the activity, erase the writing with a damp cloth and you are ready to use the patterns again.

Bulletin Board

Materials: Paper frog and lily pad shapes (patterns, page 55), pen or marker, stickers

Activity: Keep track of your students' reading progress with this motivational bulletin board! Write each student's name on a lily pad and mount it on a bulletin board along with a large frog (enlarge the pattern). Place a sticker on the lily pad each time the student reads a book. Students especially enjoy reading orally with a buddy. Add a new twist to your buddy reading by inviting another class to your "pad" to read!

Venn Diagram

Literature: *About Amphibians*, by Cathryn Sill

Materials: Venn diagram (reproducible, page 56), pencils

Activity: Review the basic characteristics of amphibians with *About Amphibians,* by Cathryn Sill. Now that your students have studied frogs, toads, and salamanders, they will be ready to organize all that new information. A Venn diagram is the perfect tool. Pick the two creatures that are vital to your unit for the students to compare. Using copies of the Venn diagram on page 56, have the students compare and contrast the characteristics of these backyard amphibians. Model for the students where to print the title for the comparison (in the pond area) and how to label the lily pads properly.

Food Chain

Literature: *Bugs for Lunch*, by Margery Facklam; *Amphibian*, by Barry Clarke

Materials: Construction paper, scissors, pencils or crayons, glue or tape

Activity: Jump-start a discussion on food by reading aloud *Bugs for Lunch,* by Margery Facklam. Children may be surprised to learn just how many animals, including toads, dine on bugs. If amphibians eat bugs, which predators get hungry for amphibians? Use the "Friends and Enemies" section of *Amphibian,* by Barry Clarke, to teach your young scientists that frogs, toads, and salamanders are an integral part of pond life and food chains. After your class has generated several food chains with your guidance, your students can demonstrate their understanding of the food chain by creating one of their own. Provide the students with strips of colorful construction paper. Each child should begin with a producer, or plant. Write the name of the producer on a construction paper strip and then continue by writing one member of the food chain on each additional strip. Include the chosen amphibian in its proper place and be sure to include one of its many natural enemies, like bats, snakes, birds, or even larger frogs. Link the strips together in order, using a bit of glue or tape to hold each paper loop in place. Display the completed projects as a visual reminder of the interdependence of the plants and animals in a food chain.

© Carson-Dellosa • CD-0584 *Learning through Literature*

Frog and Lily Pad Patterns

Venn Diagram

56

Author Ideas

Giving Words to a Classic

Literature: *Frog Goes to Dinner*, by Mercer Mayer; *A Boy, a Dog, and a Frog*, by Mercer Mayer

Materials: Paper and pencils

Activity: Put your young authors to work with two classic wordless adventures of a boy and his frog, *Frog Goes to Dinner* and *A Boy, a Dog, and a Frog* both by Mercer Mayer. After sharing the pictures and talking together about what is happening on each page, assign each child a page in the book. The child should then write or dictate a sentence or two describing the action and/or dialogue depicted on his page. Arrange the students in the order of their pages and have them share their new story orally. Bind the pages into a class book for all to enjoy!

Variation: Turn the children's versions of the stories into puppet shows. Draw pictures of the characters on heavy paper. Then color, cut out, and mount them on long rulers or craft sticks. Have the children practice reading their lines and moving their puppets while hiding behind the puppet theater. The puppet theater can be as simple as a table draped with a long tablecloth. You may choose to tape record the readings—even adding music or sound effects—to play as the children move their puppets to act out the story.

The ABC's of Amphibians

Literature: *Fantastic Frogs*, by Fay Robinson; *Australian Frogs*, by Carolyn MacLulich; *Salamanders*, by Edward Maruska

Materials: Card stock, small container, paper, pencils, crayons

Activity: Read several books about amphibians, such as *Fantastic Frogs* by Fay Robinson, *Frogs* by Carolyn MacLulich, or *Salamanders* by Edward Maruska. Each of these books offers a brief overview with simple sentence structure and photos that will captivate your audience and provide the perfect reinforcement for your unit. Now that your students have learned so much about amphibians, challenge them to create their own classroom resource—an ABC book.

First, brainstorm words and phrases that relate to amphibians and display them in the room as a guide. Write each letter of the alphabet on a card and put it in a container. Let each child choose a letter out of the container. He will be responsible for creating that page. Students can use one or more words to represent their letters. Have each student write his letter as a large capital in the corner of a sheet of paper. He will then use that letter to create a sentence about amphibians and illustrate it. Examples: "**A** is for **a**mphibians. Frogs, toads, and salamanders are amphibians." "**B** is for **b**ugs and **b**ats. Amphibians eat bugs and bats eat amphibians." Arrange all your students' work in alphabetical order and have a class reading of the ABC book. Bind the finished pages together, adding title, copyright, dedication, and "all-about-the-authors" pages.

Frogs and Other Amphibians

Story Starters

Literature: *The Mysterious Tadpole,* by Steven Kellogg; *Tuesday,* by David Wiesner

Materials: Lily pad pattern (reproducible, page 55), green paper or construction paper, white paper, pencils

Activity: Begin by reviewing story elements such as character, setting, and plot with your young readers. Then read aloud a great amphibian adventure like those mentioned below and challenge students to create adventures of their own based on the story they have just heard. The stories can be dictated to volunteers, written with invented spelling, or told in pictures. Publish the stories in books that resemble lily pads (enlarge the pattern on page 55). Parent volunteers or older student helpers can staple several sheets of plain paper between green lily pad covers.

The Mysterious Tadpole, by Steven Kellogg, is about a boy who receives what everyone believes to be a tadpole for his birthday. As it grows, it looks less like a frog and more like a giant sea creature. Have each author begin his story with the premise that he has been given his own mysterious tadpole. Encourage each writer to use his imagination and have his tadpole grow into something special.

Tuesday, by David Wiesner, is a nearly wordless book about frogs overtaking a community one night. Limp lily pads are strewn about in the morning and the townspeople are left shaking their heads in wonderment. Assign your students the role of the community members. What do they make of the lily pads? What adventure might have taken place last night? Alternatively, have several students work together to create a text for the wordless book.

Awesome Amphibian Poetry

Materials: Poetry pattern (reproducible, page 59), pencils, chart paper and marker

Activity: As a class, brainstorm a list of adjectives that describe frogs, toads, or amphibians. Record all of the students' ideas on chart paper. Students can use these descriptions to create poems about their favorite amphibians. Using the poetry pattern on page 59, your young authors can fill in the blanks with adjectives to create poems about frogs or use the same format to write poems about other amphibians. The poetry can be serious or silly. Published and decorated, these literary works can be compiled into a class book, glued into a poetry notebook, or displayed around the classroom.

© Carson-Dellosa • CD-0584 *Learning through Literature*

Awesome Amphibian Poetry

Name: _____

Frogs!

Frogs!
Frogs!
Frogs!
_____ frogs,
_____ _____ frogs,
_____ _____ _____ frogs!
_____ frogs,
_____ frogs,
_____ _____ frogs,
_____ _____ frogs!
_____ frogs, too!
_____ frogs,
_____ frogs.
Don't forget _____ frogs.
Last of all, best of all—I like _____ frogs!

Art, Music & Drama

Froggy Puppets

Literature: Let's Go Froggy series, by Jonathon London

Materials: Brown paper lunch bags, construction paper, glue, markers, wiggly eyes, crayons, felt, scissors, butcher paper

Activity: After reading a book from the Let's Go Froggy series by Jonathan London, have students make froggy puppets of their own. Using brown paper lunch bags, students can create unique frog puppets and decorate them with construction paper, markers, wiggly eyes, crayons, felt, etc. When the puppets are complete, students can form small groups and recreate the story with a retelling or simply by reading the book aloud and having the puppets do the talking. Students will really enjoy designing a scenic background on butcher paper and will be challenged by retelling the story in their own words.

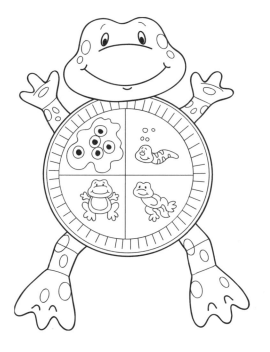

Paper Plate Life Cycles

Literature: *Tale of a Tadpole*, by Karen Wallace

Materials: Paper plates, frog pattern (page 64), crayons, scissors, glue, cotton balls and frog stickers (optional)

Activity: Using paper plates, students can recreate the life cycle of a frog or toad. Review the stages of growth by reading *Tale of a Tadpole* by Karen Wallace. Give each child a paper plate. This will become the frog's tummy. Visually divide the plate into four sections, one for each growth stage in a frog's life cycle. Students can draw, paint, or cut and paste pictures for the stages of growth. Cotton balls can also be used to represent the eggs and frog stickers can be attached to represent adult frogs. Have students cut out the adult frog's legs, arms, and head and glue them around the plate (patterns, page 64). Completed frogs can be displayed on a bulletin board or placed around the room to share with visitors what the students' have learned.

Frogs and Other Amphibians

Flashy Paintings

Literature: *Flashy, Fantastic Rain Forest Frogs*, by Dorothy Hinshaw Patent

Materials: White paper, crayons, watercolor paint, brushes

Activity: Read *Flashy, Fantastic Rain Forest Frogs*, by Dorothy Hinshaw Patent, to your class, then let the fun begin! Students will enjoy learning about these frogs from the rain forest. The exciting colors make the book interesting to look at and may inspire your young artists to paint a masterpiece.

You may choose to create a cardboard frog template. Students can trace around the rain forest template on a piece of white paper, and then use crayons to outline, but not fill in with color, a design on the frog shape. Remind students to press hard as they color with the crayons. Working on top of a folder, newspapers, or other stack of papers enables the child to press firmly and use a lot of wax without breaking the crayon. It is important to make heavy crayon lines because the wax will resist the watercolor paint in the next step.

Now that the frog has both crayon lines and white space, each student will brush the watercolor of his choice across the whole paper, being sure his brush is loaded with water. The watercolor paint will be resisted by the crayon but will fill in the white spaces beautifully. Allow the paintings to dry before cutting out the frogs. Display the paintings in your classroom to create a flashy environment.

Froggy Faces

Materials: Large, white, frog face cutouts (use an enlarged copy of pattern on page 64 to make the cutouts); paint; brushes or sponges; construction paper; wiggly eyes; markers

Activity: Give each student a large, white frog face cutout. Encourage students to paint the frog's entire face. They may choose sponge painting or finger painting to give the faces a unique texture. Some students may decide to use traditional green, while others will paint more vividly colored frogs. Allow the faces to dry overnight. Once they are dry, the eyes and tongue can be added by gluing on construction paper cutouts or large wiggly eyes. Permanent markers will also work on the dried paint if students wish to incorporate additional features.

Once the faces are complete, they can be used in many different ways. Display them in the classroom or tape them to sticks and use them in a puppet show. Another idea is to use the finished faces to publish work such as poetry or amphibian reports. Students can copy their writing onto the backside of the faces and then tape the faces to rulers. Children will enjoy holding up their froggy faces as they share their work aloud.

Create Your Own Wetland Habitat

Literature: *In the Small, Small Pond*, by Denise Fleming; *The Salamander Room*, by Anne Mazer

Activity: Read aloud *In the Small, Small Pond*, by Denise Fleming, and *The Salamander Room*, by Anne Mazer. Both of these stories will help your students learn what features make up a habitat, specifically a pond. Over a few days, your students can work together to design and produce their own wetland habitat!

Pond
Cut a large piece of blue butcher paper—as large as the table or counter on which your habitat will be displayed. Trim the edges in a wavy shape to resemble water. Take your students on a rock hunt around the school grounds. The fist-sized rocks they find can be placed around the edge of the "pond."

Water Lilies
Materials per student: 6 white paper leaves, approximately 6 in. x 2 in. (15 cm x 5 cm); 10 to 15 white or yellow tissue paper squares, about 1 in. (2.5 cm) in size; one 3 in. (7.5 cm) paper circle, any color; dish or plate of glue, crayon

Directions: Using an almond-shaped pattern, each student cuts six white leaves. Paste the leaves around the paper circle to create a flower. Give each table of students a handful of tissue paper squares. To make the center blossom, each child should wrap a square of tissue paper around the blunt end of a crayon. Dip this end into the glue and press it to the flower center. Continue until the flower center is covered with tissue paper. Now each child has created a blossoming water lily. Place the finished lilies around the pond.

Grass
Materials: Green construction paper, scissors, glue, rocks

Directions: Ponds have lots of reeds and grasses growing along the edges and so should yours! Give each student a long piece of green construction paper about 2 in. (5 cm) wide. Have the students fold their papers in half lengthwise. Folding the paper grass allows it to stand straight and tall. Now the student can trim the folded piece to a point toward the fold at the top. Fold the bottom up about 1 in. (2.5 cm). Put glue on this bottom edge and secure the edges to the butcher paper pond. It looks best when the grasses are glued in small clusters in just two or three areas around the pond. If the grasses are falling over you can support them with the rocks your students found on the rock hunt.

Birds' Nests
Materials: Brown paper lunch bags, green cellophane grass

Directions: Birds' nests are often found in and among the reeds of a wetland habitat. To create a nest, simply roll down the edges of the bag until you have a bowl-shaped nest. Fill each nest with green cellophane grass. Place several nests in the midst of the reeds along the edge of the pond.

© Carson-Dellosa • CD-0584 *Learning through Literature*

Frogs and Other Amphibians

Insects

Materials: Chewy candy insects or small plastic insect toys

Directions: Much to a frog's delight, lots of insects make their homes around a pond! Sprinkle a handful of chewy candy insects around your habitat. Save some as a treat for your young naturalists for building such a unique wetland habitat! Alternatively, you could use small plastic toy insects to populate your habitat.

Amphibians

Directions for salt-dough amphibians can be found in the recipes section (see page 65). Use these creations to provide amphibians for your pond or use toy animals.

Paper Plate Life Cycles Pattern

Fun Recipes

Frog Leg Cookies

Literature: *Gilbert de la Frogponde: A Swamp Story*, by Jennifer Rae

Materials: Sugar cookie dough, green candy sprinkles or green colored sugar

Activity: Students may reject the idea of eating actual frog legs, but will certainly be tempted to taste this sweet version! Begin the cooking lesson by reading *Gilbert de la Frogponde,* by Jennifer Rae. In it, a fat, lazy frog must convince two chefs that frog legs really are not very tasty but insects surely are. After an appetizing discussion about eating our favorite amphibians, challenge your chefs to create their own frog leg delicacies. You can use any sugar cookie recipe or purchase premade dough.

After students have washed and dried their hands, give each student a handful of the cookie dough. Have them divide their dough into three or four smaller pieces. Each piece can now be molded into the shape of a frog's leg. (You may want to draw a large example on the chalkboard.) Encourage students to roll out the dough beneath their palms like a snake. Then, by squeezing one end a little thinner and bending it slightly, they can easily transform the dough into a frog leg. Dust each pale leg with green sprinkles or colored sugar. Place the finished legs on cookie sheets, label them so kids can eat their own creations, and bake according to recipe directions. What a tasty treat!

Salt-Dough Amphibians

Materials: 2 parts flour, 1 part salt, 1 part water, 1 part sawdust or oatmeal (optional for lumpy toads), tempera paints, brushes

Activity: In a large bowl, mix together these ingredients with your hands. If the dough is wet and tacky, add more flour until it becomes dry like clay. Give children lumps of the salt dough and remind them it is not for tasting! Each student can mold his dough into the shape of a frog or a salamander. Allow the dough to dry overnight. Now your artists can use tempera paints to decorate the amphibians. After the paint has dried, these clay creations will add the finishing touch to your wetland habitat (see page 62)!

Math

Leapfrog Math

Materials: Measuring tape, chalkboard and chalk or chart paper and marker

Activity: Put a unique twist on this childhood favorite! Establish a baseline from which children will jump. One at a time, have each student crouch down at the baseline and, like a frog, leap up and out. Another child can use a measuring tape to measure the jump. Keep track of the distances jumped on the chalkboard or chart paper.

Once every child has had one or two turns of leaping, record the results on a graph. Then, use the graph to practice problem solving with your class. How many students jumped a distance greater than 2 feet? Which two distances jumped had an equal number of students? How many more students jumped 3 feet than 4 feet? Of course, your questions will differ based upon the results shown in your graph.

Variation: If time does not permit a whole class jumping session, divide the students into pairs. Give each pair space to jump, a measuring tape, and a recording sheet. One member of the pair can leap while the other measures and records. Distances can then be reported to the whole class.

More Graphs

Students love to create pictographs. Not only do they get a chance to vote, but they also create the symbols that are used to represent the information. There are many ways to incorporate pictographs into this amphibian unit. Some examples include:

- Graph favorite amphibian stories. Give each child a book cutout on which to write his favorite book title.
- Graph favorite amphibians. Each child can illustrate and cut out her favorite.
- Vote on story endings. Before reading the end of a story, elicit predictions from the class. Have your audience vote on the most likely ending with a name badge on the graph.
- Have the children pretend they are amphibians and vote on what they consider to be the most appetizing food.
- If the students were amphibians, where would they like to live—in a pond, at the zoo, in the rain forest? Elicit other suggestions from your young experts.

Use these graphs to practice solving problems like those mentioned in the previous activity. Display the finished graphs in the hallway for all to enjoy!

© Carson-Dellosa • CD-0584 Learning through Literature

At-Home Activities

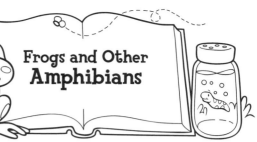

Sequencing and Retelling Backpack

Literature: *Jump, Frog, Jump!* by Robert Kalan

Materials: Backpack, parent letter (top of page 68), pictures or plastic toys representing animals from the story, sentence strips, a copy of *Jump, Frog, Jump!*

Activity: Pack a backpack with the parent letter on page 68, the book *Jump, Frog, Jump!* by Robert Kalan, and pictures or plastic toys representing the animals from the story that can be used for sequencing and retelling. Puppets or small stuffed animals would also work nicely.

Before you begin, write the events of the circular story on sentence strips. This story makes use of many animals from the wetlands habitat and is perfect practice for sequencing events. Then share the story. After the oral reading, conduct a whole class lesson on sequencing using the sentence strips you have prepared. Lead the children to discover how easy an oral retelling is once the main events have been put in the proper order. Call on several students to retell the story. Finally, show the students the backpack you have prepared and discuss your expectations.

The students are to read the story aloud to a family member and use the animals to sequence the story's events first and then to retell *Jump, Frog, Jump!*

Personal Time Line

Materials: Personal Time Line Project Sheet (reproducible, bottom of page 68)

Activity: As they have worked through the activities in the amphibian unit, students have had much practice in reading and creating time lines. They are now able to identify the stages of growth in a frog's life and put them in sequential order. Extend the time line lesson by having each child create a time line of her own. Send home a copy of the Personal Time Line Project Sheet on page 68, which explains the directions for the project. Before you describe the project to your class, prepare an example time line so the children can clearly see your expectations. As noted in the Assessment section in the Introduction (see page 5), if you plan to grade this project make sure the students understand the rubric before they begin work on their time lines.

Sequencing and Retelling Backpack

Dear Parents,

Our class loved reading *Jump Frog Jump!* in class. This book's wonderful representation of a food chain in a wetlands habitat is given in a playful manner that young children enjoy. These backpack activities will not only strengthen your young reader's comprehension skills but will support oral language development as well. Thank you in advance for assisting your child with these activities.

Directions for the student:

1. Read *Jump Frog Jump!* aloud to an adult.
2. Use the animals to put the story events in order from beginning to end.
3. Retell the story using your own words. The animals will help you.

Please return the backpack and all its contents to school by _____. Thank you for your continued support!

      Sincerely,

Personal Time Line Project Sheet

Due Date _____

Your job is to create a time line of your life. Just like an amphibian goes through stages of growth, so do you! Think about important events that have happened in your life. You took your first step. Maybe you have already lost a tooth. Perhaps you broke a bone. Were you a part of a wedding? Do you remember your first Halloween costume? You might have learned to ride a bike. Consider all the exciting things that you have already done!

Your time line should include one significant event for each year of your life. Display at least one picture for each occasion. You can use photos, drawings, or cutouts. Poster board or construction paper can be used to create your time line. Be prepared to talk about your time line because you will present it to the class. Get your family involved with this project; they may remember details that you don't. Be creative and have fun!

Insects and Spiders

Young students love to learn about insects and spiders. In this section, we share a variety of fiction and nonfiction literature selections that capture students' interest in bugs. Tap into your students' creativity with quilting ideas, clay bugs, edible spiders, and shape books. Include parents in student learning with backpack ideas and parent letters.

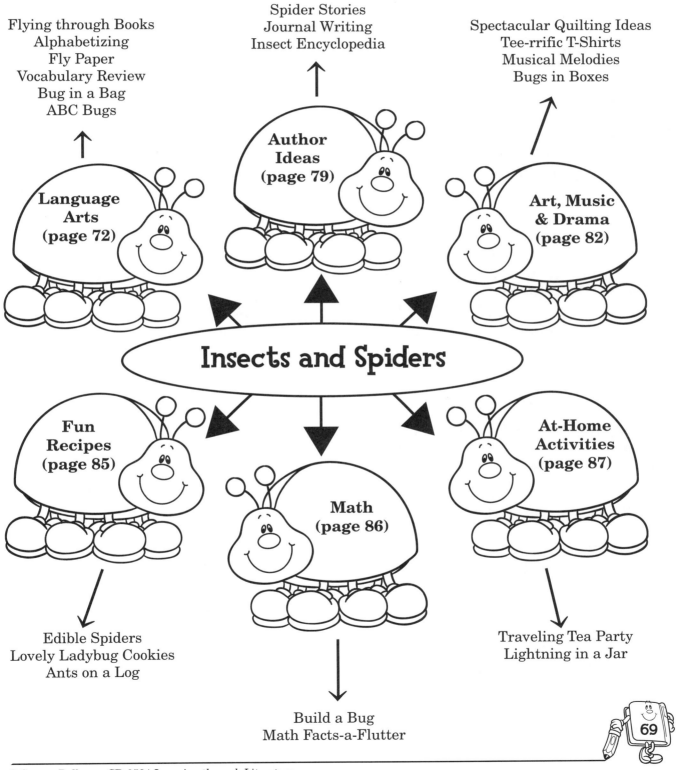

Flying through Books
Alphabetizing
Fly Paper
Vocabulary Review
Bug in a Bag
ABC Bugs

↑

Language Arts (page 72)

Spider Stories
Journal Writing
Insect Encyclopedia

↑

Author Ideas (page 79)

Spectacular Quilting Ideas
Tee-rrific T-Shirts
Musical Melodies
Bugs in Boxes

↑

Art, Music & Drama (page 82)

Insects and Spiders

Fun Recipes (page 85)

Edible Spiders
Lovely Ladybug Cookies
Ants on a Log

Math (page 86)

Build a Bug
Math Facts-a-Flutter

At-Home Activities (page 87)

Traveling Tea Party
Lightning in a Jar

© Carson-Dellosa • CD-0584 *Learning through Literature*

Literature Selections

Featured Literature

The following selections are used in conjunction with the activities in this section. You may want to obtain them from your library before you start the unit. (Activities with which the books are used are listed in parentheses.)

Nonfiction

Bugs! Bugs! Bugs! by Bob Barner (Chronicle Books, 1999). This easy-to-read introductory story about a variety of bugs uses rhyme and descriptive adjectives. (Tee-rrific T-shirts, page 83)

The Icky Bug Alphabet Book, by Jerry Pallotta (Charlesbridge Publishing, 1986). Pallotta uses accurate facts and beautiful illustrations to present bugs from A to Z. (ABC Bugs, page 73)

Fiction

Butterfly, by Susan Canizares (Scholastic Inc., 1998). An ugly cricket wishes to be a beautiful butterfly. This story suggests that there is beauty in all creatures as friends share what they enjoy about the cricket's qualities. (Flying through Books, page 72)

The Itsy Bitsy Spider, by Iza Trapini (Charlesbridge Publishing, 1997). Many children may be familiar with the "Itsy Bitsy Spider" song, but this book extends it. The spider goes up the water spout as well as exploring many other places. Music is included in this favorite. (Spider Stories, page 79)

Miss Spider's Tea Party, by David Kirk (Scholastic, 1994). This delightful picture book is filled with bright, colorful illustrations that tell a story in verse. (Traveling Tea Party, page 87)

More Bugs in Boxes: A Pop-Up Book about Color, by David Carter (Simon & Schuster Books for Young Readers, 1990). Carter uses bugs to teach colors in this fun pop-up book. (Tee-rrific T-Shirts, page 83; Bugs in Boxes, page 84)

Old Black Fly, by Jim Aylesworth (Holt, 1992). This alphabet story written in rhyme shares the adventure of a fly and his humorous, annoying visits around the house. The pictures are bright and colorful and illustrate beautifully the chaos caused by one pesky fly until . . . splat! (Fly Paper, page 72)

The Very Quiet Cricket, by Eric Carle (Philomel Books, 1990). A very quiet cricket meets many interesting friends during his search for his voice. The book uses repetition, which helps your audience share in the discoveries. What a great sound surprise at the end for all young listeners! (Musical Melodies, page 84)

When Lightning Comes in a Jar, by Patricia Polacco (Philomel Books, 2002). This is a charming story about children who gather with relatives at a family reunion. All day long, the children look forward to catching lightning in a jar. Finally, at nightfall, the children use jars to catch lightning bugs. (Lightning in a Jar, page 87)

© Carson-Dellosa • CD-0584 *Learning through Literature*

Additional Suggested Literature

Nonfiction

Bugs, by Nancy Winslow Parker and Joan Richards Wright (Mulberry, 1987). Simple rhyming question-and-answer pages are followed by detailed information on a variety of insects and other creepy-crawly creatures.

Have You Seen Bugs? by Joanne Oppenheim (Scholastic, 1999) Beautiful torn-paper illustrations and simple text examine the variety of bugs and their habitats.

The Icky Bug Counting Book, by Jerry Pallotta (Charlesbridge Publishing, 1992). Pallotta uses bugs as the subjects to learn about and count from 1 to 26 in this wonderful alphabet book.

Fiction

Benjamin's Bugs, by Mary Morgan (Bradbury Press, 1994). There is so much to see and do as Benjamin's curiosity leads his exploration with his mother.

Hey Little Ant, by Philip and Hannah Hoose (Tricycle Press, 1998). This whimsical dialogue between a boy and an ant is written in rhyme for fun oral reading. The ending leaves it up to the readers to decide the fate of the ant.

Sam's Sandwich, by David Pelham (Dutton Children's Books, 1991). A wide variety of creepy crawly insects is used as Sam builds a sandwich for his sister. The pages unfold for the reader to guess and see the insects as each layer is built to make a tasty sandwich filled with surprises.

Ten Little Ladybugs, by Melanie Gerth (Piggy Toes Press, 2000). Children can reinforce counting backwards as ten bugs disappear one by one. This books contains illustrations with ladybugs that can be easily counted.

Two Bad Ants, by Chris Van Allsburg (Houghton Mifflin, 1988). Two ants desert their colony and find dangerous adventures in a kitchen.

The Very Hungry Caterpillar, by Eric Carle (Philomel Books, 1994). A hungry caterpillar eats his way into becomimg a beautiful butterfly. This book reinforces days of the week and number recognition.

The Very Lonely Firefly, by Eric Carle (Philomel Books, 1995). As a firefly searches the night sky for other lightning bugs, there are many lights that mislead him on his journey. This book is especially fun to read in dim light so young listeners can enjoy a bright surprise ending.

Why Mosquitoes Buzz in People's Ears: A West African Tale, retold by Verda Aardema (Dial Press, 1975). This award-winning book attempts to explain why mosquitoes whine in our ears to this day!

Zzzng! Zzzng! Zzzng! A Yoruba Tale, retold by Phyllis Gershator (Orchard Books, 1998). This retelling shares a story about a mosquito that sets out as a small irritation of joyful singing and becomes a real pest.

© Carson-Dellosa • CD-0584 *Learning through Literature*

Language Arts

Flying through Books

Literature: *Butterfly*, by Susan Canizares

Materials: Construction paper, scissors, pencils or crayons

Activity: Share the book *Butterfly*, by Susan Canizares, with the class. This activity lets students demonstrate their ability to summarize the story and identify story elements. Have each student create a butterfly out of construction paper. On each of the wings, students can identify the parts of the story found in the book. Make materials available to them if children want to create butterfly summaries of other books they have read. Then hang the finished butterflies on a bulletin board to promote student-selected literature as well as display their artwork.

Alphabetizing

Materials: Caterpillar section pattern (reproducible, page 74), construction paper, glue

Activity: Alphabetizing is an important new skill in the primary grades. Give each student a set of caterpillar sections (pattern on page 74) and have him write a different letter of the alphabet (or word) on each segment. Allow students time to cut out and glue the circles onto construction paper in alphabetical order. (Teachers can easily adapt this concept for math by having students sequence numbers.)

Fly Paper

Literature: *Old Black Fly*, by Jim Aylesworth

Materials: Fly pattern (reproducible, page 75), pencils

Activity: Give each student a paper fly (pattern, page 75) on which you have written a letter from the alphabet on one wing. The child should then write one or more words that begin with that letter on the other wing. Variations could include having the student write words that end with the given letter or has the letter sound in the middle of the word. One great book to use with this activity is *Old Black Fly*, by Jim Aylesworth.

Insects and Spiders

Vocabulary Review

Materials: Reproducibles (pages 76–78), pencils

Activity: Whether students are enjoying reading bug books for pleasure or they are learning more about insects in science, it is a good idea to familiarize students with vocabulary words related to bugs and their definitions.

Using the open reproducibles on pages 76–77, plug in words and/or definitions. Write words, facts about insects, etc. below the pictures on page 76 or cut apart the cards and write phrases on the back of each insect. Students could also be asked to identify terms by coloring in certain recognized words (on the flowers on page 77). You can provide the words and directions to fit your lesson objectives. Complete page 78 by listing spelling words you would like students to practice.

Bug in a Bag

Materials: Books about bugs, magazines with pictures of bugs, toy plastic bugs, brown paper bags

Activity: Provide an opportunity for your students to learn more about insects and spiders. This can take place in several ways: read books about insects aloud to the children, have them read to one another. Take the time to discuss what the students have learned, encouraging them to use descriptive language.

Without allowing the students to watch, put plastic bugs in brown paper bags. Have the students carefully describe what they feel in the bags and then ask other students to guess which toy bugs are hidden.

ABC Bugs

Literature: *The Icky Bug Alphabet Book*, by Jerry Pallotta

Activity: Read *The Icky Bug Alphabet Book*, by Jerry Pallotta, and discuss other insects that could be used for each letter in this alphabet book. Test students' memory skills by playing this game. Begin by saying, "I'm going on a nature walk and I'm taking an . . ." Start with a bug that begins with an A (ant). The next child repeats the phrase and the A bug and adds a B bug (beetle), and so on through the alphabet.

© Carson-Dellosa • CD-0584 *Learning through Literature*

Alphabetizing Pattern

Fly Paper Pattern

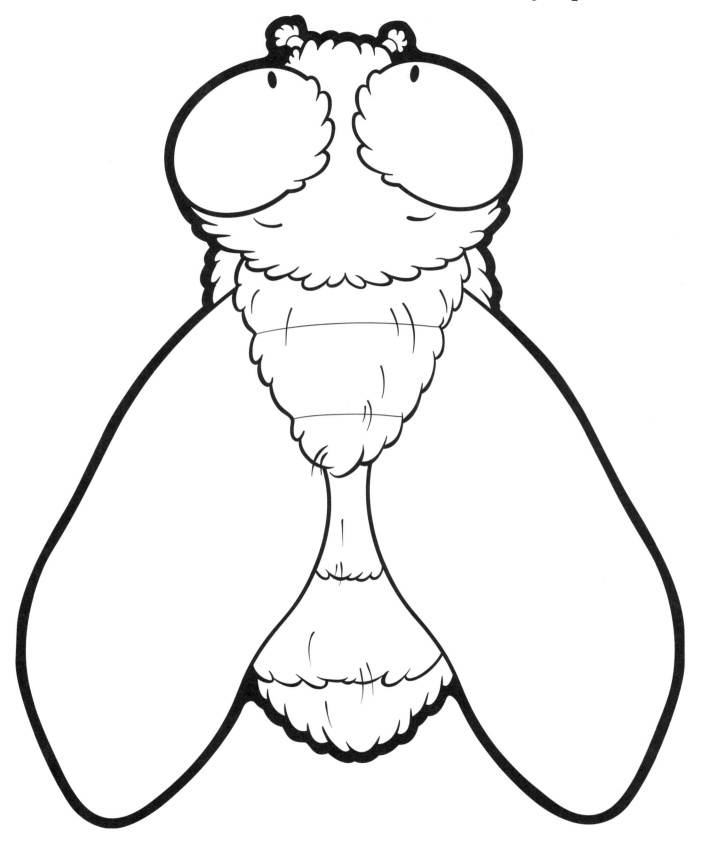

75

Vocabulary Review

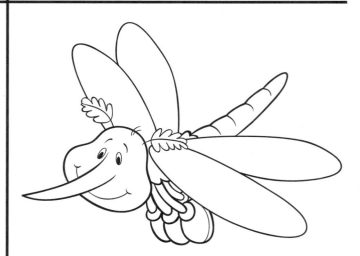

Vocabulary Review

Name: _____ Date: _____

Directions: _____
_____
_____

Vocabulary Review: Buggy Spelling List

Name: _____ Date: _____

1. _____
2. _____
3. _____
4. _____
5. _____
6. _____

Author Ideas

Insects and Spiders

Spider Stories

Literature: *The Itsy Bitsy Spider*, by Iza Trapini

Materials: Paper plates, white paper, stapler, black construction paper, scissors, chenille craft stems, wiggly eyes, pencils or crayons, yarn or string, glue

Activity: After reading *The Itsy Bitsy Spider*, by Iza Trapini, children will love writing spider stories in these spider shape books. Using a paper plate as the back cover, staple 14 blank white pages to the paper plate (staple at the top only). Cut a black piece of construction paper to fit on top of the blank pages and staple it to the book. Students can transform their books into spiders by stapling eight chenille-stem legs to the paper plate. Provide wiggly eyes to complete the spider books. On each page (using both sides of the pages), students can write the name of a bug, working through the alphabet.

You could also use a spider-shaped book as a class book in which each student writes one page. The page could be a retelling, a description of a favorite insect, or a spider fact. Hang completed spiders from the students' desks or from the ceiling by long pieces of yarn or string.

Journal Writing

Materials: Student journals, pencils

Activity: Daily writing experiences give children an opportunity to practice using written lanuage to express their feelings about things. After sharing both fiction and nonfiction books about bugs, give children time to record their thoughts in journals. Perhaps students could have a few minutes each day to write, or maybe you could select one or two days a week to designate as journal days. Some writing prompts could include the following: A Day in the Life of an Ant; The scariest bug of all is…; If I were a bug, I would be a . . . ; One day the spider awoke to find a _____ trapped in her web!

Insect Encyclopedia

Materials: Construction paper, stapler, pencils, butterfly pattern (reproducible, page 80), Buggy Book List (reproducible, page 81)

Activity: Use the reproducible pattern on page 80 to make a class booklet about insects. Staple sheets of construction paper as a cover. As your class studies insects, each student can illustrate a page in the booklet by drawing the insect on the left side of the butterfly and list facts about the assigned bug on the other half of the butterfly's body. Alternatively, students can create individual booklets by illustrating and writing about insects on plain sheets of paper, which are collated into a booklet.

Facts could include what the bug eats, its size and color, where the bug lives, what eats the bug, how the bug moves, the bug's life span, and other interesting information. Students can record the books that they have read on the Buggy Book List reproducible found on page 81.

Insect Encyclopedia Reproducible

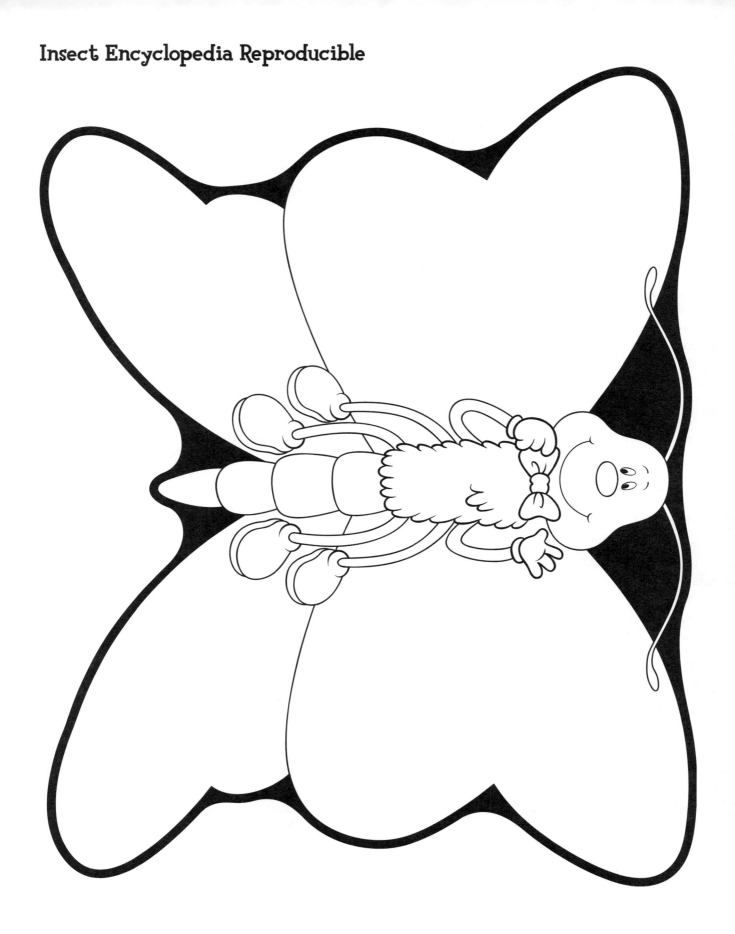

Buggy Book List

Name: _____ Date: _____

Title	Author	Genre

Art, Music & Drama

Spectacular Quilting Ideas

Materials: 12 in. (30 cm) fabric and paper squares (white or other light colors work best), fabric paint in various colors, newspaper, cardboard, buttons, ribbons, fabric pens, colorful backing material, sewing machine, pencils, glue, tape

Activity:

1. Before beginning this project, you may want to schedule several parent volunteers, particularly those with sewing or quilting experience, to help during the course of the students' work.

2. Provide each student with a fabric square and a paper square. Students should leave a 1 in. (2.5 cm) border around the edge of each square (this is where the squares will be sewn together). A cardboard border template could be made from old boxes and used to block off the margin.

3. Choose a work area where the finished work can remain undisturbed for 24 hours. Cover the work area surface with newspapers. Place a cardboard form on top of each square and tape that securely to the surface. Now you have set up your students for success. The fabric squares will not move and the borders will ensure that the students' designs do not go too close to the edge. Before students go to the quilting work area, have them draw their insects with pencils on the paper squares. These drawings will serve as their rough drafts and you will be able to make suggestions before they commit their designs to paint. Some students may need to be reminded to make their insects large enough so that when the quilt is done, everyone can stand back and enjoy the beauty and differences of the bugs.

4. When students have completed their pencil drawings, they may go to the quilting work area where their fabric squares are secured and matted. They should then use their pencils to draw their bugs on the fabric. After the outline of a bug is drawn using pencil, the student can redraw it using various colors of fabric paints (markers or tubes with tips on them).

5. When the fabric square has a bug neatly drawn on it and the colors have been added, allow each work of art to dry for about 24 hours before moving it. All of your students will probably not be able to paint in one day, but the project can easily be completed in a few days or up to a week.

6. Once the students have completed their squares, the quilt can be put together. Students can help to design the quilt by placing their squares in a pattern on the floor. If the squares are uneven in number, you may want to add some blank squares. You could use one of the blank quares to give the quilt a title panel. Alternatively, children's names could be added to the blank squares.

7. Sew the squares together to create the front panel of your quilt. Now, a backing must be added to the sewn squares. When selecting backing material, you may want to look for colorful material that fits the theme of the quilt. The backing will need to be larger by 2 in. (5 cm) on each side than the completed front panel. This edge can be turned over the front panel's edge to give your quilt a colorful border. Sew the colorful backing to the front panel. Fancy buttons and ribbons can be added to the completed quilt.

Insects and Spiders

Tee-rrific T-shirts

Literature: *More Bugs in Boxes: A Pop-Up Book about Color*, by David Carter; *Bugs! Bugs! Bugs!* by Bob Barner

Materials: Plain white T-shirt for each child, fabric pen, white paper, pencils, fabric paint, wiggly eyes and hot glue (optional)

Activity: Making T-shirts is a fun way to share with others what your students are learning, unite your class, and motivate them to learn even more about the topic. Ask each student to bring in a plain, white T-shirt. Be sure to have them write their initials on the tags before you collect them. You will want to have a T-shirt for yourself and it is a good idea to have a few extra on hand for students who neglect to bring one.

Prior to starting the project, decide if you want the students to make realistic bugs or make-believe bugs. Keep in mind, not all students are artists. Make-believe bugs allow room for error.

The first step is to remind students of various insects they have studied and what makes them unique—colors, shapes, legs, eyes, wings, antennae, etc. A class discussion is a great way to review. List the ideas on the chalkboard or chart paper. Share the book *More Bugs in Boxes* by David Carter. *Bugs! Bugs! Bugs!* by Bob Barner is another great book to use to give children ideas for drawing their own bugs. Students can create the bugs intended for their T-shirts on plain white paper. (Refer to page 101 for a sandpaper variation of this project.) Encourage students to draw their bugs big! Students should share their final sketches with you so that you may edit the designs and make suggestions prior to committing the designs to the T-shirts.

Place cardboard inside the T-shirt and have each student draw his sketch neatly on the T-shirt using a pencil. Pencil marks are difficult to erase on the fabric, so it is recommended that students draw lightly.

Once students are satisfied with their sketches, they can make their bugs come to life by adding color with fabric paint. You may want students to use the fabric paints to outline their insects, or they can paint using a different color each day, allowing the paint to dry before adding a new color, to avoid the paints mixing together.

After students have completed their paintings, final touches may be added. One option is to hot glue wiggly eyes to the T-shirts to create eyes for the insects. You may want to plan on having a T-shirt day when all students are encouraged to wear their buggy T-shirts to school! (Don't forget yours!) What a great way to express the fun and learning that is happening in the classroom.

Insects and Spiders

Musical Melodies

Literature: *The Very Quiet Cricket*, by Eric Carle

Materials: Recordings of instrumental music, cassette or CD player, papier-mâché materials, old lightbulbs, paint and brushes

Activities: Bugs are fabulous creatures to which to listen. Each insect has a movement or a beautiful sound it creates that is unique to its species. Introduce this concept with Eric Carle's book, *The Very Quiet Cricket*. Name a specific insect or spider. Play some instrumental music and ask students to move around the classroom silently acting and moving as the bug identified. (Example: Butterflies fly gracefully so your students should move gracefully around the room gently "flapping" their arms as if flying. Spiders walk on lots of legs; students can crab walk around the room using both arms and legs.)

Invite the students to create sounds made by bugs. To begin, cover a lightbulb with papier-mâché. Once the entire lightbulb has a thick coating of papier-mâché, allow it to dry. Then gently tap the lightbulb and the interior glass will break. The lightbulb could then be painted to represent one of the noise-making bugs. Shake the lightbulb like a rattle to make sounds of crickets, katydids, cicadas, and grasshoppers.

Bugs in Boxes

Literature: *More Bugs in Boxes: A Pop-Up Book about Color*, by David Carter

Materials: Modeling clay, paint, brushes, markers, shoe boxes, glue, scissors, construction paper

Activity: Read *More Bugs in Boxes,* by David Carter, to the students. Provide students with clay and ask them to create bugs of their own. After the clay has dried, have your students add details with paint and markers. You may wish to take the project one step further. Give each student a shoe box and the materials she needs to create a habitat for her insect.

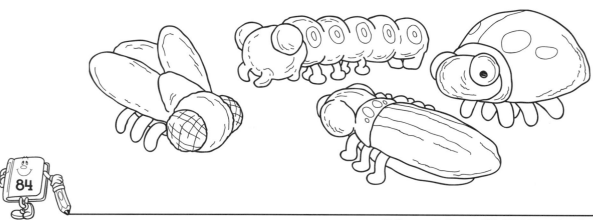

Fun Recipes

Insects and Spiders

Edible Spiders

Materials for each spider: One large marshmallow, 8 small pretzel rods, 2 miniature candy-coated chocolate pieces for eyes, peanut butter

Activity: Add the eight legs (small pretzel rods), four onto each side, by sticking them carefully into the marshmallow body. Eyes can be affixed with a dab of peanut butter spread (if students are not allergic to the food) on the back of the chocolate candies.

Lovely Ladybug Cookies

Materials: Tube of sugar cookie dough, oven, cookie sheet, knife, red frosting, chocolate baking chips, black or red licorice strings, candy eyes (from bakery or specialty store, optional)

Activity: Cut chilled cookie dough into individual slices and then bake the round cookies following the directions on the packaging. After the cookies have cooled, allow students to decorate their own ladybug cookies using red frosting. Students can add chocolate chips for spots and black or red licorice strings for antennae. (If desired, you may purchase candy eyes at a baking specialty store.)

Variation: At your directions, students can add odd or even numbers of spots to review this skill. They will be easy to "spot check" for accuracy!

Follow-Up Activity: A follow-up discussion can be held to review vocabulary and facts relating to insects, highlight prior knowledge about ladybugs, and—if you wish to do this—build interest in hatching ladybugs in the classroom. Generate a class list of the basic needs of most insects (e.g., water, food source, etc.). Here are some possible questions for discussion: Why do ladybugs have spots? Are all ladybugs red with black spots? How long does a ladybug live? What are some other names for the ladybug? Challenge your students to find the answers in reference books.

Ants on a Log

Materials: Peanut butter, celery, knife, raisins, plastic knives

Activity: Invite students to make "ants on a log." Wash the celery and cut it into approximately 4 in. (10 cm) pieces. Students can use plastic knives to spread peanut butter on the celery and then place a few raisins ("ants") on top. Note: Substitute with other foods if students are allergic to peanuts.

Math

Build a Bug

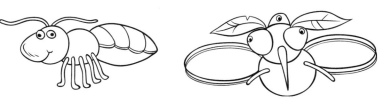

Materials: Drawing paper, water-based markers or pencils

Activity: Have your students combine their creativity with their math skills! Ask each student to draw a bug with 12 body parts. The student can decide how many body segments, how many legs, how many eyes, how many wings, and how many antennae her bug will have. The final product is up to the child as long as the total number of body parts equals 12. (To reinforce how many body parts true insects and spiders have, share pictures of bugs with the children.)

Variations: Have students work in groups. Groups can randomly select from a bag a number that indicates how many body parts the group needs to create on the bug. Once each group has created its bug, display the bugs and have the class determine the number of body parts the group needed to include by counting the bug's body parts orally together.

Bugs also can be built using beads, felt pieces, feathers, chenille craft stems, wiggly eyes, foam rubber pieces, scraps of fabric and construction paper, packing peanuts, etc. Students will need glue and scissors and plenty of space to be creative!

Math Facts-a-Flutter

Materials: Construction paper, pencils, scissors, crayons, tape, watercolor paints, brushes

Activity: Students often can have an easier time remembering math rules when the rules are applied to a visual. For example, fact families have three numbers (members of the family) that are written in four different math sentences.

Ask each student to create the body of a butterfly on white construction paper. Be sure the student creates the body with a head, thorax, and abdomen (three parts in all). Then have the student write the three members (three numbers) of the family, one on each main body part (head, thorax, and abdomen). You may wish to assign a different fact family to each student.

Now, students can create the four beautiful wings! First, have them draw the four wings and cut them out. Using the three members of the math family, ask students to write a math sentence on each wing. Before they begin to color and outline the math sentences, they should raise their hands so their sentences can be checked. Once they have used the three numbers correctly in four sentences, have students attach the wings to their butterfly bodies with tape on the back. Encourage students to color fancy designs on their butterflies' wings. Then, using watercolor paints, they can paint over the crayon marks, creating a crayon resist and a gorgeous, lasting memory of math facts.

The butterflies can be displayed on a bulletin board or in the hallway to create a real "flutter" for school friends to enjoy!

Variation: Have the students write their related math sentences on copies of the reproducible butterfly pattern (page 80) and display them in the classroom.

© Carson-Dellosa • CD-0584 *Learning through Literature*

At-Home Activities

Insects and Spiders

Traveling Tea Party

Literature: *Miss Spider's Tea Party*, by David Kirk

Materials: Backpack, copy of *Miss Spider's Tea Party*, parent letter (reproducible, page 88), decaffeinated tea bags (optional), chart paper, water-based marker, 12 plastic bugs (optional)

Activity: School can be much more fun and exciting when families get involved and learning can continue at home. So, why not provide parents with the tools to help motivate and enhance student learning? Here's how!

Read *Miss Spider's Tea Party*, by David Kirk. Discuss how the book is written in rhyme and how the book can be read with rhythm. Model the technique by sharing the book again. Have students identify the pattern and beats. Print short examples of the verse on the chart paper using symbols to show the rhythm used. After the book is familiar to your students, place the book into a backpack. Also enclose a copy of the parent letter (page 88), filled in with your directions about how to read the book. As an added touch, place two decaffeinated tea bags in the backpack so parents and their child can celebrate reading the book with a tea party.

Students, rotating turns, can take the backpack home to share with parents and siblings. Students will have fun with the literature and can practice rhythms, rhymes, and beats while they review the story. Encourage parents to return the backpack to school with their child the next day. Then the rotation can continue and all students will have the opportunity to take the backpack home.

Counting can also be reviewed if you include 12 plastic bugs inside the backpack. (You might purchase the plastic spider rings that are sold around Halloween when they are relatively inexpensive and easy to find.) As the story is read, students can add spiders to a tabletop one by one as the creatures are introduced throughout the story.

Lightning in a Jar

Literature: *When Lightning Comes in a Jar*, by Patricia Polacco

Materials: Copy of *When Lightning Comes in a Jar*, craft materials (ribbons, buttons, felt, paint pens, etc.), clear plastic jars, parent letter (reproducible, page 88)

Activity: Foster family activities and reading for pleasure with Patricia Polacco's book, *When Lightning Comes in a Jar*. Children will enjoy this book about catching lightning bugs in a jar on a summer night. Send the book home for students and their parents to read together. You can also include materials like ribbons, buttons, felt, paint markers, etc., so children can decorate their own lightning bug jars. Enclose a letter to parents explaining the activity and how it ties into your study of insects in the classroom. (See the open parent letter reproducible on page 88.)

At-Home Activities Letter

Date _____

Dear Parent(s),

We have been learning about our tiny friends, the insects and spiders. You can help us continue to learn more about them at home, and here's how!

_____
_____
_____
_____
_____
_____
_____
_____
_____
_____

As always, thank you for your continued support. Working together makes learning more fun!

                        Sincerely,

My Body

Students will be delighted with the activities included in this section. Fiction and nonfiction books are used as springboards for writing exercises, small group and individual projects, and exciting activities the class completes together. From the five senses to our skeletal system, these activities will make learning about the body fun.

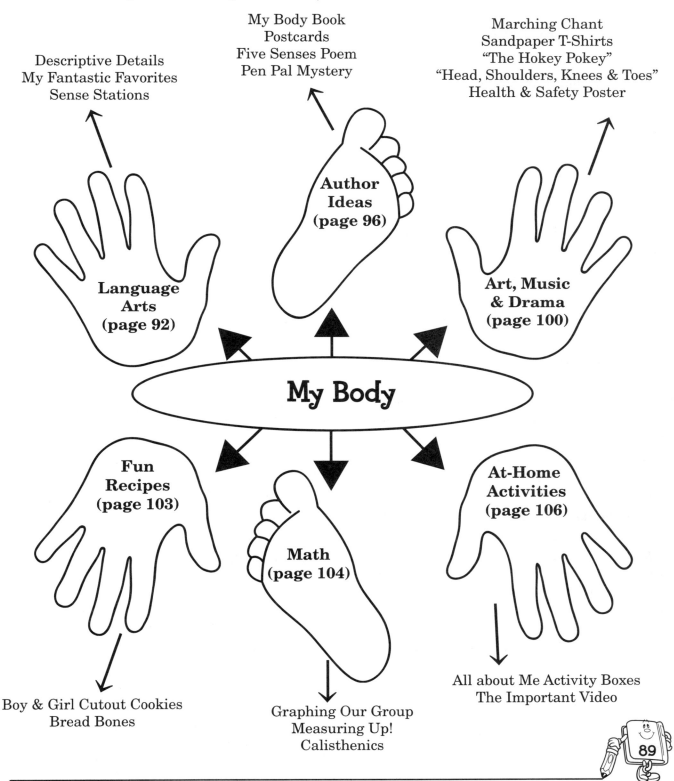

Descriptive Details
My Fantastic Favorites
Sense Stations
↑
Language Arts (page 92)

My Body Book
Postcards
Five Senses Poem
Pen Pal Mystery
↑
Author Ideas (page 96)

Marching Chant
Sandpaper T-Shirts
"The Hokey Pokey"
"Head, Shoulders, Knees & Toes"
Health & Safety Poster
↑
Art, Music & Drama (page 100)

My Body

Fun Recipes (page 103)
↓
Boy & Girl Cutout Cookies
Bread Bones

Math (page 104)
↓
Graphing Our Group
Measuring Up!
Calisthenics

At-Home Activities (page 106)
↓
All about Me Activity Boxes
The Important Video

Literature Selections: My Body

Featured Literature

The following selections are used in conjunction with the activities in this section. You may want to obtain them from your library before you start the unit. (Activities with which the books are used are listed in parentheses.)

Nonfiction

Bones, by Stephen Krensky (Random House, 1999). This simplified look at the human skeleton is a perfect choice for the youngest readers. (Bread Bones, page 103)

Germs Make Me Sick! by Melvin Berger (HarperCollins, 1996). Bacteria and viruses are simplified and demystified in this charming book about being sick. The topics of getting better and preventing illness are also included. (Health & Safety Poster, page 102)

The Happy Book, by Diane Muldrow (Scholastic, Inc., 1999). This touch-and-smell book presents simple pleasures like mittens, fur, the smell of cocoa, etc., to inspire discussion about the senses. (My Fantastic Favorites, page 92)

I Can Move, by Mandy Suhr (Carolrhoda Books, 1992). An easy-to-read overview of how skeletons allow children to run, jump, and play. A skeleton labeled with primary vocabulary is included. (Bread Bones, page 103)

It's Okay to Be Different, by Todd Parr (Little, Brown, 2001). Each page and picture express the importance and fun of being different. (Descriptive Details, page 92)

Me and My Amazing Body, by Joan Sweeney (Crown Publishers, 1999). Told in story form from the point of view of a little girl, the simple text introduces the parts of the body, including skin, heart, and muscles. (Sandpaper T-shirts, page 101)

My Amazing Body: A First Look at Health and Fitness, by Pat Thomas (Barron's, 2002). Thomas presents a simplistic look at the amazing body and how food and exercise are key components to staying healthy. Several questions are presented for discussion. (Marching Chant, page 100)

My Five Senses, by Aliki (Crowell, 1962). This classic picture book provides an excellent introduction to sight, sound, taste, smell, and touch. (Sense Stations, page 93)

My Five Senses, by Margaret Miller (Simon & Schuster Books for Young Readers, 1994). This book shares photographs of children naming things pleasant and not so pleasant, like flowers and garbage, that your five senses can detect. (Five Senses Poem, page 97)

Your Insides, by Joanna Cole (Putnam & Grosset, 1992). This book provides a great overview of the skeleton, muscles, nerves, and major organs in terms young learners can easily understand. Includes four plastic overlays of the body's systems. (My Body Book, page 96; Sandpaper T-shirts, page 101)

Fiction

A Bad Case of Stripes, by David Shannon (Blue Sky Press, 1998). Shannon uses humorous illustrations and a nonsense story to explore the anxiety and fears many students experience at the beginning of a new school year. (All about Me Activity Boxes, page 106)

My Body

The Hokey Pokey, by Larry LaPrise, Charles Macak, and Taft Baker (Simon & Schuster Books for Young Children, 1996). The words to this popular song and dance are written and illustrated with pictures of many children grooving to the beat. ("The Hokey Pokey," page 101)

I Love You the Purplest, by Barbara M. Joosse (Chronicle Books, 1996). Two little boys share the day fishing with their mother. Each boy inquires who is the best and tries to get her attention and love. The patient mother tenderly answers each question, stating that one is very good for one reason, but the other is very good for another reason. (Boy & Girl Cutout Cookies, page 103)

The Important Book, by Margaret Wise Brown (Harper, 1949). Brown uses the same pattern on each page to describe the most important things about common objects. (The Important Video, page 107)

Jessica's X-Ray, by Pat Zonta (Firefly Books, Ltd., 2002). Jessica breaks her arm and takes a trip to the hospital. Students will enjoy this factual story about bones. Actual x-rays are included. (Postcards, page 96)

Additional Suggested Literature

Nonfiction

Human Body, by Claude Delafosse and Gallimard Jeunesse (Scholastic, 2000). This nonfiction book briefly touches on many aspects of the body, like bones and the five senses. This perfect introduction contains several plastic overlays.

A Rainbow of Friends, by P. K. Hallinan (Ideals Children's Books, 1994). This picture book is written in easy-to-read rhyme. All friends are special and everyone is accepted is the premise for this beautiful book.

The Way I Feel, by Janan Cain (Parenting Press, Inc., 2000). Written in rhyme with colorful, fun illustrations, this picture book leads young readers through the variety of feelings we all have. Each feeling is written in a style to resemble the emotion that helps to emphasize the feeling.

Fiction

More Parts, by Tedd Arnold (Dial Books for Young Readers, 2001). In this story, a young boy becomes nervous when he hears idioms about body parts, such as a broken heart and jumping out of your skin. (Sequel to *Parts*. See below.)

My Many Colored Days, by Dr. Seuss (Alfred A. Knopf, 1996). Colors represent feelings in this picture book written by Dr. Seuss. The illustrations reflect both color and emotion and tie in beautifully with Dr. Seuss's rhyming text.

Parts, by Tedd Arnold (Dial Books for Young Readers, 1997). Told in rhyme, this hilarious story is about a little boy who fears he is falling apart. He notices stuff coming out of his nose, his comb has several hairs in it, and the skin around his toes is peeling.

My Body

Language Arts

Descriptive Details

Literature: *It's Okay to Be Different*, by Todd Parr

Materials: Reproducible (page 94), pencils

Activity: Students become increasingly aware of the differences between themselves and their classmates as they get older. What makes us different also makes us unique and is what makes us who we are. Read the wonderful children's book, *It's Okay to Be Different*, by Todd Parr, to your class. In the book, the author expresses the importance of accepting our differences and the beauty of our uniqueness.

Assign student pairs and give each student a copy of the reproducible on page 94. Ask your students to record descriptive words or adjectives that describe their bodies as well as those of their partners. (Examples: blonde hair, blue eyes, two feet, etc.) Encourage students to color and add favorite outfits to represent themselves, then display the completed papers in your classroom.

Variation: Providing your students with fabric, felt, yarn, and buttons will turn these projects into three-dimensional sensations!

My Fantastic Favorites

Literature: *The Happy Book*, by Diane Muldrow

Materials: Reproducible (page 95); pencils; large, paper hand-shaped cutouts

Activity: Your students will begin to think about things that make them happy as you read *The Happy Book*, by Diane Muldrow, to your class. This lift, scratch, and sniff book takes students through many treasured sights, smells, and memories! Provide your students the opportunity to visit their own wonderful memories, created from their five senses, and encourage them to write about these memories so they last a lifetime! Begin by giving each student the reproducible on page 95. Have the students complete each of the five lines, filling in their favorite sights, sounds, tastes, smells, and textures. Students can later transfer their ideas (after you have edited their work for spelling errors) individually to a large cutout hand, writing one line on each finger.

My Body

Sense Stations

Literature: *My Five Senses*, by Aliki

Read *My Five Senses*, by Aliki, to your students as a great review of sight, sound, touch, taste, and smell. Then set up the two "sense stations."

Touch

Materials: Cardboard box with a lid, wrapping paper, sharp knife, items that have a variety of textures (e.g., feather, rabbit's foot, cotton balls, sandpaper, rock, rubber ball, etc.), science journals, pencils

Activity: Create a "feely box" out of any cardboard box with a lid. Begin by wrapping the box with colorful paper. Use a knife to cut a hole in the middle or at one end of the box. The hole should be big enough for a student's hand to fit through it. Fill the feely box with several items that have a variety of textures. Attach the lid. Leave the feely box at a table along with a basket of pencils and science journals. Children can visit the center, reach into the feely box, and grasp an item. Without looking at it, have them describe in their journals exactly what they are feeling and then attempt to name each item. Later, after each student has had a chance to complete the activity, reveal the hidden items. Praise students for correct responses and close attempts.

Variation: Put several different textured items in a large sack. Group your class in a circle. Choose one student to reach into the bag and grasp one item. She then describes what she is feeling to the group. Can other students guess what it is? After an item has been revealed, remove it from the sack so it will not be chosen again.

Smell

Materials: Empty film canisters, substances with different fragrances (peppermint, peanuts or peanut butter, flowery perfume, baby powder, coffee, chocolate, cinnamon, citrus fruit, pumpkin, black licorice, or anything that carries a strong aroma), permanent marker, cotton balls

Activity: Collect a group of empty film canisters. Put a different fragrance in each canister and use a permanent marker to number the cap on each. Set up the collection at a table along with numbered recording sheets and a can of pencils. Invite children to sniff one scent at a time and then write beside its number on the sheet what they suspect it is. Reveal the identity of the scents after everyone has had a chance to visit the station.

Notes:
- Make sure to check for student allergies when choosing substances for the canisters.
- The best way to capture a fragrance is to douse a cotton ball with the liquid carrying the scent.
- Check the spice rack at your local grocery store for more ideas.

Descriptive Details

Name: _____

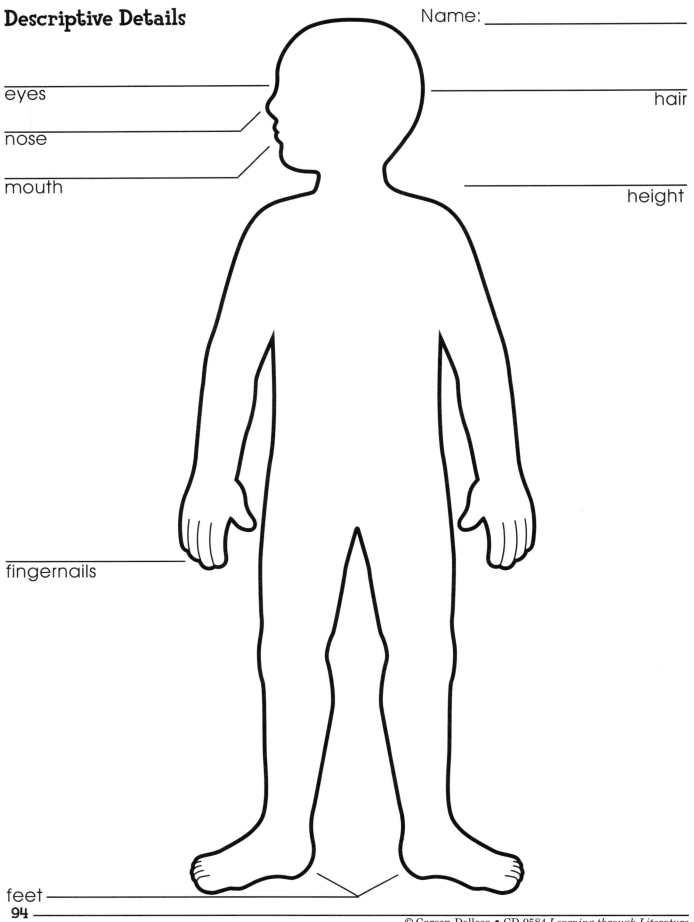

eyes _____

nose _____

mouth _____

hair _____

height _____

fingernails _____

feet _____

My Fantastic Favorites

Name: _____
Date: _____
My favorite sights: _____
_____
My favorite sounds: _____
_____
My favorite things to feel: _____
_____
My favorite things to taste: _____
_____
My favorite things to smell: _____
_____

- -

My Fantastic Favorites

Name: _____
Date: _____
My favorite sights: _____
_____
My favorite sounds: _____
_____
My favorite things to feel: _____
_____
My favorite things to taste: _____
_____
My favorite things to smell: _____
_____

Author Ideas

My Body Book

Literature: *Your Insides*, by Joanna Cole; *Me and My Amazing Body*, by Joan Sweeney; or other simple factual books about the body

Materials: Booklets made of pages with a simple body outline between construction-paper covers (one for each student), pencils, crayons

Activity: Begin your unit on the body with a read-aloud that will preview the major organs, bones, and muscles. Two examples are *Your Insides*, by Joanna Cole, and *Me and My Amazing Body*, by Joan Sweeney. Both of these nonfiction books discuss the body in a way that a young audience will understand and enjoy. Next, create a booklet entitled "My Body Book" for each child by assembling several pages that contain a simple body outline between construction-paper covers. Each lesson you cover about the body deserves an illustration and an entry in the book. For example, after you discuss the location and function of the brain, students can draw a brain in the head of the body and write a simple sentence about it on the facing page. Other entries can include the heart, lungs, stomach, five senses, nerves, muscles, and bones. What a great reference!

Postcards

Literature: *Jessica's X-Ray*, by Pat Zonta

Materials: White drawing paper, black construction paper, scissors, white chalk, pencils

Activity: Give your students a taste of what it is like to go to the hospital with a broken bone by reading *Jessica's X-Ray*, by Pat Zonta. Guide a discussion of how Jessica may feel throughout the ordeal and reinforce the knowledge students gained about X rays and bones. Follow up your discussion with a postcard writing activity. Have your students pretend to be Jessica. Cut sheets of white paper into fourths and give each student one piece for a "postcard." As Jessica (or "Jess" for boys), each student will write a postcard to Grandma and Grandpa (or another relative) telling them all about the broken-bone experience. Mount the postcard onto a same-sized piece of black construction paper. The black side will be the picture side of the postcard. Give each author a piece of white chalk. The student can then use the chalk to draw an X ray of the part of the body mentioned in the postcard. What beautiful bones!

© Carson-Dellosa • CD-0584 *Learning through Literature*

My Body

Five Senses Poem

Literature: *My Five Senses*, by Margaret Miller

Materials: Reproducible (page 98), pencils, chalkboard and chalk or chart paper and marker, individual cups of ice cream (optional)

Activity: A five senses poem is one that describes an object or an event using a simple form that includes sight, smell, sound, touch, and taste. See the open form on page 98. Review the senses by reading aloud *My Five Senses*, by Margaret Miller. This simple picture book uses photographs to remind us that some things we sense are pleasant and cheerful, like flowers, but some are rather unpleasant, like garbage or dirty socks!

Begin by choosing an item with which everyone is familiar, like ice cream, to write about as a class. Write the names of the five senses on the board or on separate pieces of chart paper. Elicit words from your class that describe ice cream using their five senses. (Giving the students individual cups of ice cream would make the task easy and fun!) Next, use the brainstormed words to compose a group poem orally. After the class has written the ice cream poem together, you can either have them write their own ice cream poems individually or give them a new topic to brainstorm as a class.

After modeling the class poem, most students are capable of writing their own if you continue to brainstorm the words together. This takes the pressure off of those students who insist they can think of nothing to write. A good topic that is effortless for children is the current season or an upcoming holiday. Generate the words to describe the event and record them on chart paper. Then give each child a copy of page 98. These poems along with students' illustrations will certainly brighten up a bulletin board.

Pen Pal Mystery

Materials: Pen Pal Mystery Cards (reproducible, page 99), pencils, classroom mailboxes or cubby holes

Activity: Encourage your students to share information about their interests and what makes them unique and reinforce their writing skills at the same time! You can encourage your entire class to become writers simply by having each student respond to the reproducible on page 99.

Invite students to fill in their responses independently without identifying themselves on their papers. Collect the responses and place them randomly in classroom mailboxes or student cubby holes. Students then try to guess by reading the filled-in information, the identities of their pen pals. Each student can read her mail orally to the class and then try, within three guesses, to identify her mystery pen pal.

© Carson-Dellosa • CD-0584 *Learning through Literature*

Five Senses Poem   Name: _____

I see _____ .

I hear _____ .

I smell _____ .

I taste _____ .

I feel _____ .

Five Senses Poem   Name: _____

I see _____ .

I hear _____ .

I smell _____ .

I taste _____ .

I feel _____ .

Pen Pal Mystery Cards

Dear Pen Pal,

Hello! I would like to introduce myself to you!

I am _____ years old. I have _____ hair and my eyes are _____.

I really like _____. My favorite color is _____ and I love to eat _____. When I grow up I want to be a _____. I live with my _____ in a _____.

Can you guess who I am?

Dear Pen Pal,

Hello! I would like to introduce myself to you!

I am _____ years old. I have _____ hair and my eyes are _____.

I really like _____. My favorite color is _____ and I love to eat _____. When I grow up I want to be a _____. I live with my _____ in a _____.

Can you guess who I am?

Art, Music & Drama

Marching Chant

Literature: *My Amazing Body: A First Look at Health and Fitness*, by Pat Thomas

Activity: Read *My Amazing Body: A First Look at Health and Fitness*, by Pat Thomas, to make students aware of the importance of physical activity. They will discover that food and exercise are key components to staying healthy. Reinforce that message with the marching chant below. Recited like a military marching chant, say each line and then have the children repeat it. (The first and last syllable of each line is accented.) Add movement by marching your class around the playground or in place inside your classroom, as you chant the rhyme. Challenge older students to come up with new couplets about the body and keeping it healthy. Now that's music to your ears!

> Healthy living is the best.
> Put your body to the test.
> Healthy living makes me tick.
> Germs can really make me sick.
> Cover your mouth when you cough or sneeze.
> Wash your hands if you please.
> Exercise can make me strong.
> Sitting around all day is wrong.
> Try to eat a balanced meal.
> You'll be amazed at how you feel.

© Carson-Dellosa • CD-0584 *Learning through Literature*

My Body

Sandpaper T-shirts

Literature: *Your Insides*, by Joanna Cole; *Me and My Amazing Body*, by Joan Sweeney

Materials: Plain white T-shirt for each student, permanent marker or laundry marking pen, sandpaper, a large supply of old crayons, old newspapers, iron and ironing surface

Activity: About one week before this project, ask each student to bring in a plain white T-shirt. Be sure to have a few extras just in case. Label each with its owner's name on the tag. When all of the students have brought in their shirts, read *Your Insides*, by Joanna Cole, or *Me and My Amazing Body* by Joan Sweeney, to get an overview of the organs inside the chest.

Next, each young artist will draw and color the heart, lungs, and stomach on pieces of sandpaper, which will be ironed onto the T-shirts. Give each child three pieces of sandpaper, each about 5 in. (12 cm) square. Encourage children to press hard with their crayons as they color one organ on each piece of sandpaper. The sandpaper really eats up the crayons so try to use old ones. Working on top of a stack of newspapers makes it easier to press firmly without breaking the crayons.

When the coloring is finished, enlist a few adult volunteers to help iron. Place cardboard inside each T-shirt so the wax will not bleed through to the back. Assist the child in placing each piece of sandpaper face down in the approximate location of the real organ. Iron on medium-high, dry heat for 60 to 90 seconds. Peel up one corner to check if the color is transferring to the shirt. Allow the sandpaper to cool slightly, then carefully peel it up. Plan a day toward the end of your unit for each student to wear her T-shirt to school. What a great review for organ location!

"The Hokey Pokey"

Literature: *The Hokey Pokey*, by Larry LaPrise, Charles Macak, and Taft Baker

Material: Recording of "The Hokey Pokey"

Activity: Read *The Hokey Pokey*, by Larry LaPrise, Charles Macak, and Taft Baker. This simple song provides great inspiration for the body unit! Not only does it review body parts and right and left directions, but it also encourages physical activity! Get your students up and moving with a recording of this classic favorite.

My Body

"Head, Shoulders, Knees & Toes"

Materials: Sentence strips and marker

Activity: Use this classic song as an introduction to body parts. Write the words to this tune on sentence strips and invite the students to mimic your movements as you point to each body part. Next, change the words to review other body parts. For example, you could sing another stanza using eyes, elbows, hips, and ankles. Yet another stanza could include nose, wrists, thighs, and calves.

Health & Safety Poster

Literature: *Germs Make Me Sick!* by Melvin Berger

Materials: Chart paper and marker, large sheets of construction paper, crayons or markers

Activity: Many children in your class may have had colds by this time in the school year. In fact, they most likely passed it around to one another right there at school. Begin by asking students about colds, how they are spread, how you feel when you have a cold, and what the symptoms are for a cold. Read *Germs Make Me Sick!* by Melvin Berger. Bacteria and viruses are made simple to understand in this picture book.

Follow up a lesson on preventing illness with this art project. Begin by charting ways we can all keep from getting and spreading germs. Next, give each child a large piece of construction paper. Have him write a slogan across the top that encourages others to prevent illness, like "Wash Your Hands Often" or "Cover Your Mouth when You Cough." Students can refer to your chart for help. Encourage students to illustrate their posters with drawings of people following or not following health and safety rules. Share the finished posters orally and hang them around the school to remind all students to keep their germs to themselves!

Fun Recipes

Boy & Girl Cutout Cookies

Literature: *I Love You the Purplest*, by Barbara M. Joosse

Materials: Sugar cookie dough, rolling pin, waxed paper, flour, cookie cutters or templates resembling a boy and a girl, cookie sheet(s), refrigerator, oven, a variety of colored frosting for clothes and hair, candy-coated chocolate pieces for eyes, candy sprinkles, tube frosting for fine details (mouth, buttons, pockets, etc.)

Activity: Review the body's parts and how everyone comes in their own package! Discuss how some of us are taller or shorter, or that some of us have yellow hair, brown hair, or no hair. Read *I Love You the Purplest*, by Barbara Joosse, with your class and discuss people's similarities and differences. This book is a loving story sharing the relationship between a mother and her two sons and how each boy is a special gift with unique qualities. After reading the book with your class, discuss the story and then ask students to reflect on what makes them special.

This activity allows students to create their bodies with cookie dough and see how everyone is different. Make sugar cookie dough (or buy dough in the refrigerated section of your grocery store) and provide students with cookie cutters or templates that resemble a boy and a girl. Students will enjoy rolling out the dough and cutting out a body shape. Place the cutout shapes on a cookie sheet (labeled with students' names on parchment paper) and store them in the refrigerator at school; then you can bake the cookies at your convenience. Once the cookies are baked, provide your students with all of the edible ingredients it will take to let them create truly unique cookies that resemble them! (Alternatively, you could provide students with cookies that have already been baked and simply let the children decorate the cookies to personalize them.)

Bread Bones

Literature: *I Can Move*, by Mandy Suhr; *Bones*, by Stephen Krensky

Materials: Bread dough; cookie sheet; oven; jelly, peanut butter, or honey (optional)

Activity: Enjoy the books *I Can Move*, by Mandy Suhr, and/or *Bones*, by Stephen Krensky, with your class to reinforce the importance of our skeletal system. Small groups will use bread dough to construct bones in the skeletal system. You may choose to use your favorite recipe for bread or simply buy bread dough in the refrigerated section at the local market. Each group will need its own batch of dough. It is a good idea to have at least one poster of the human skeleton for the students to use as reference. Groups will then use their dough to create the major bones of the skeleton on a cookie sheet.

After washing their hands, students can divide the dough into small pieces and roll it under their palms to make snake-like shapes, forming the ends to look like real bones. As they finish each bone, they should lay it right on a cookie sheet (to label bones write student's name on parchment paper) so it is ready to bake in the oven. Bake according to package or recipe directions. Once the bread bones are baked, students can use their creations as a reference or enjoy them as a tasty treat! If you decide to eat the bread bones, you may want to provide jelly, peanut butter, or honey as a spread.

Math

Graphing Our Group

Materials: Paper and pencils or chart paper and marker

Activity: Allow your students the opportunity to reflect on their body attributes with this activity that combines health and math. Students can visualize how they are the same as their classmates and how they differ. Individuals can create their own graphs or this can be a wonderful teacher-directed activity, especially for younger students. If you choose to lead the class in making one graph, display it in the classroom or the hallway. Everyone will enjoy seeing your students' graphed results!

Ask students to identify their eye color, hair color, and so on, by raising their hands when each choice is announced. Then have a class recorder indicate with a tally mark the number for each attribute on a classroom tally sheet. Let students work as individuals or in a group to create graphs, or use chart paper and a marker to make a class graph.

Measuring Up!

Materials: Rulers, pencils, paper

Activity: Review the markings on a ruler (inch or half-inch will depend upon the capabilities of your class). Pair up your students so they can help measure each other and record the data. Begin with a whole class demonstration. Model measuring your hand from your wrist to your middle fingertip. Announce your hand's length. Have the students measure their hands just as you did and record their answers on pieces of paper. Use the sharing time to practice math vocabulary like *less than*, *greater than*, *odd*, and *even*. Ask questions like, "Whose hand is greater than 4 in. (10 cm) in length?" "Whose hand is less than 7 in. (18 cm) in length?" "Whose hand's length is an even number of inches (centimeters)?" Announce and model the next body part to measure, the foot. Continue measuring, sharing, and comparing the length of each student's forearm, calf, ear, and nose.

© Carson-Dellosa • CD-0584 *Learning through Literature*

My Body

Calisthenics

Activity: Practice counting and get some exercise with this activity. When your students are finishing up another activity and have been in their seats for a while, loudly announce that they need an exercise break. Remind them that exercise gets the heart pumping, which sends more blood to their limbs and organs, which will wake them up. Stand in front of your class and ask the students to spread out and to do what you do. Begin by counting to ten slowly while doing an easy exercise like making large arm circles. Students should count along with you as they perform the exercise. Next, try counting by tens while touching your toes. Finish the exercise session by counting by twos to twenty while doing jumping jacks. Students will have their math skills reinforced while taking a much needed activity break. Try to work this two-minute exercise routine into your schedule at least twice a week.

Extension: Once your students no longer need practice counting by ones, twos, fives, or tens, try counting to ten in different languages. You call out a number in Spanish, for example, and, while exercising, they repeat the number. Your students will be bilingual and fit in no time!

© Carson-Dellosa • CD-0584 *Learning through Literature*

My Body

At-Home Activities

All about Me Activity Boxes

Literature: *A Bad Case of Stripes*, by David Shannon

Materials: Empty tissue boxes (collected using the reproducible form on page 108), decorative craft materials (paper, tissue paper, sequins, crayons, etc.), glue, scissors, parent letter (page 108)

Activity: Request that students bring in empty tissue boxes from home beginning about one month before you intend to present this project to your class. This will allow plenty of time for you to have enough empty tissue boxes for each student to select one. Send home the request form on page 108 informing parents of this upcoming project.

Share the wonderful book *A Bad Case of Stripes*, by David Shannon, with your class and give your students the opportunity to discuss their likes and dislikes, special interests, pets, hobbies, and so on.

For this activity, each student will prepare an empty tissue box that will then be filled at home. Allow each student to select a box and offer plenty of materials to use to cover and decorate the outside of the boxes. Be sure each student has his name displayed clearly on the box (a photo of the student could also be used and would add an individual touch). Encourage students to decorate the sides of the tissue boxes to reflect their interests (e.g., using their favorite colors, pictures of animals found in magazines, craft jewels, favorite places to visit, or favorite seasons).

Send the decorated boxes home with the reproducible letter to parents found on page 108. Invite students and their family members to place small objects inside the box—such as special pictures of family, friends, and pets; homemade treasures; souvenirs from trips; and so on—to help give insight into what makes the child unique.

Your students will then enjoy bringing in and sharing information using the items in the box to help narrate their presentations. This activity also helps the teacher get to know the students' backgrounds and common interests and allows students opportunities to see differences and build self-worth.

© Carson-Dellosa • CD-0584 *Learning through Literature*

The Important Video

Literature: *The Important Book*, by Margaret Wise Brown

Materials: Chalkboard and chalk or chart paper and marker, student page (reproducible, page 109), video recorder and videotape, large resealable plastic bags, "ticket" (reproducible, page 110), microwave popcorn, construction paper or other material for book cover

Activity: Read *The Important Book*, by Margaret Wise Brown, to your students. Explore the language pattern Brown uses on each page and identify the pattern on the chalkboard or chart paper. Explain that you will use Brown's pattern as a model for a class book and ultimately create a video of the book. Provide the reproducible on page 109 so the students can use Brown's pattern to create a book page about the most important things about themselves. You may even want to demonstrate the process by composing your own page. For example:

> The most important thing about Mrs. Smith is that she has a wonderful family.
> She likes pizza and apples.
> She has a dog named Chester.
> She enjoys spending time on the beach.
> But the most important thing about Mrs. Smith is that she has a wonderful family.

Have students create illustrations to go with their texts. After students have completed the reproducible on page 109, they could share their work by reading their pages on videotape and holding their drawings up to display their pictures. (Alternatively you may want to use a scanner to scan each page and create a digital slide show on the computer. There are a variety of easy presentation software programs that accept scanned images and allow users to add music or narration. If your computer has a video output port, you can then export your slide show to a videotape by connecting the video output to a VCR.)

Either way you decide to create your videotape, you may want to make several copies. Place a copy of the video in a resealable plastic bag with a ticket (see page 110) and a package of microwave popcorn. What parent could resist taking a few moments to cuddle up on the couch to enjoy an evening treat and a video starring his or her child?

After your video is completed, assemble the student pages into a book and add a cover or select a student to design a book cover. Your students will enjoy this new addition to your classroom library!

All about Me Boxes

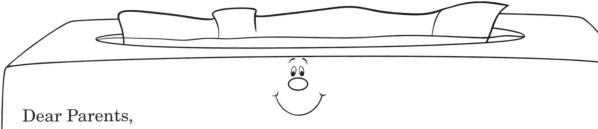

Dear Parents,

We are looking forward to getting to know our classmates better by sharing more information about ourselves, and we could use your help! Please send in empty tissue boxes (any size). We need all the boxes by _____. Our "All about Me Box" activity will begin in class, as we will decorate the boxes before bringing them home to be filled. More information about how you can help your child complete this project will be sent home along with the decorated box later in the month.

Thanks in advance for your assistance in sending in empty tissue boxes!

Sincerely,

Dear Parents,

We appreciate all of the tissue boxes that were sent in! With your help, we were able to create "All about Me" boxes that we decorated in class. Please help us complete this project at home and send your child's box back to school by _____.

Have your child place a minimum of five objects inside the box. Objects should reflect interests, hobbies, special characteristics, favorites, etc., that help describe your child. These objects can be photos, pictures cut from magazines, souvenirs, etc. Have fun helping your child express what he or she feels is important.

Thank you for your continued support.

Sincerely,

The Important Video

The most important thing about _____ is
_____.

She/he likes _____.

She/he has _____.
             (family, pets)

She/he enjoys spending time _____
_____.
                     (hobbies)

But the most important thing about
_____ is _____
_____.

The most important thing about _____ is
_____.

She/he likes _____.

She/he has _____.
             (family, pets)

She/he enjoys spending time _____
_____.
                     (hobbies)

But the most important thing about
_____ is _____
_____.

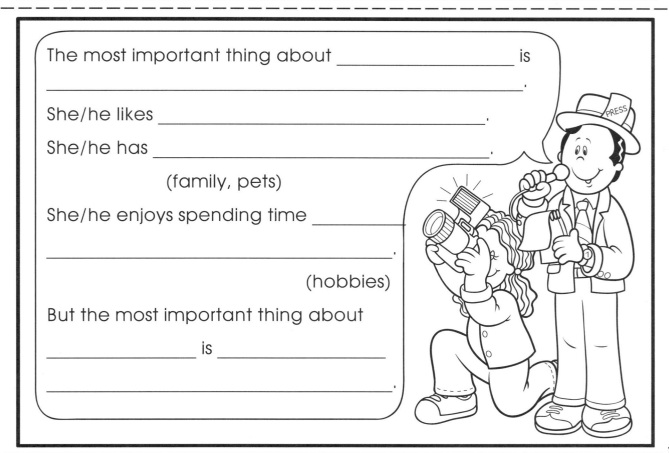

The Important Video Tickets

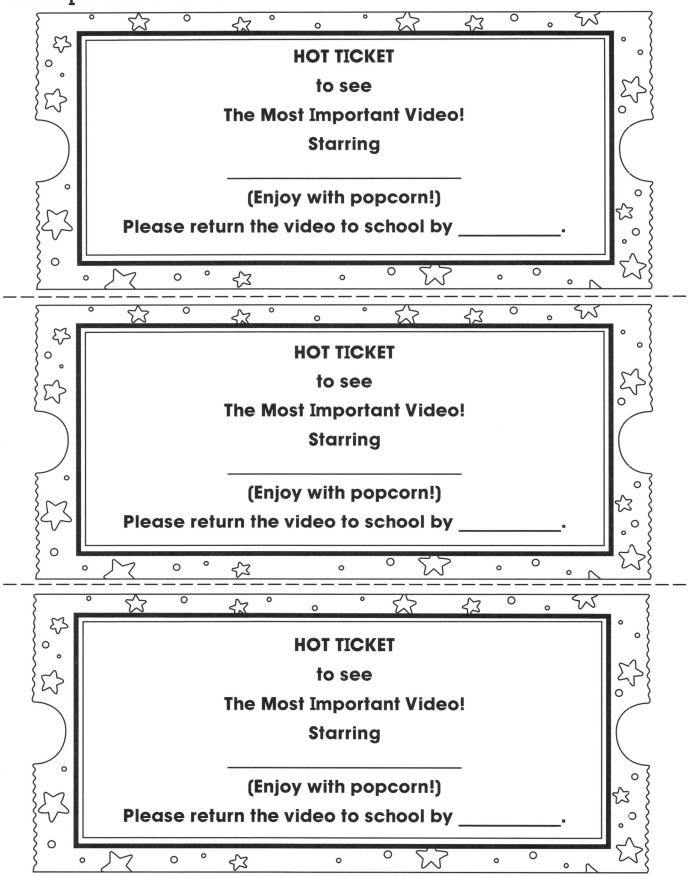

Plants and Trees

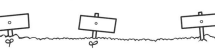

Young children love learning how plants grow and they look forward to becoming gardeners themselves. As you can see by this concept map, your students will get plenty of practice growing seeds, observing the life cycles of plants, cooking, counting, and creating art projects.

Life Cycle Flowchart
Story Pies
Picture This!
Take a Hike!
Observation Terrariums
Grow Your Own Experiments!

The ABC's of Plants
Tree-mendous Books!
Shape Books
Descriptive Writing
Haiku

Singing the Cycle
Plant Posters
A Tree-mendous Hotel
Seed Mosaics
A Tree for All Seasons

Language Arts (page 115)

Author Ideas (page 119)

Art, Music & Drama (page 122)

Plants and Trees

Fun Recipes (page 124)

Math (page 125)

At-Home Activities (page 127)

Eat Dirt!
Cooking Vegetable Soup

A Nature Walk to Count On
Counting on Seeds
A Sweet Idea
Calling All Barbers!

Autumn Leaves Backpack
Planting Reading & Retelling Skills

© Carson-Dellosa • CD-0584 *Learning through Literature*

Featured Literature

The following selections are used in conjunction with the activities in this section. You may want to obtain them from your library before you start the unit. (Activities with which the books are used are listed in parentheses.)

Nonfiction

Autumn Leaves, by Ken Robbins (Scholastic Press, 1998). This book is an easy-to-read reference for many types of leaves. (Descriptive Writing, page 120; Autumn Leaves Backpack, page 127)

Cactus Hotel, by Brenda Z. Guiberson (Henry Holt & Company, 1991). This nonfiction book tells the journey of a saguaro cactus from birth to death. Desert animals use the mighty cactus as both food and shelter. (A Tree-mendous Hotel, page 122)

From Seed to Plant, by Gail Gibbons (Holiday House, 1991). This is a simple yet informative book that explains how plants grow from seeds. Its easy-to-read text is perfect for beginning readers. (Story Pies, page 115)

From Seed to Sunflower, by Gerald Legg (Franklin Watts, 1998). Large illustrations and simple text present the life cycle of the sunflower. (Planting Reading & Retelling Skills, page 127)

A Gardener's Alphabet, by Mary Azarian (Houghton Mifflin, 2000). This alphabet book provides a great review of gardening terms from arbor to zucchini. (The ABC's of Plants, page 119)

Pumpkin Circle: The Story of a Garden, by George Levenson (Tricycle Press, 1999). Combined with stunning photography, the nonfiction text takes the reader through the entire growing cycle of a pumpkin seed in a backyard pumpkin patch. From seed to vine to jack-o'-lantern and then back to the earth, the reader can easily follow the rhyming text. Growing and harvesting tips are presented in the back of the book. (Life Cycle Flowchart, page 115)

Tell Me, Tree: All about Trees for Kids, by Gail Gibbons (Little, Brown, 2002). Gibbons presents a simple but thorough introduction to tree parts, types, and identification. Tree-mendous Books, page 119)

This Is the Sunflower, by Lola M. Schaefer (Greenwillow Books, 2000). Cumulative verse explains the life cycle of the sunflower. (Singing the Cycle, page 122; Plant Posters, page 122)

The Tremendous Tree Book, by Barbara Brenner and May Garelick (Four Winds, 1979). The rhyming text provides a great introduction to the study of trees. (Take a Hike! page 116)

Fiction

The Big Red Apple, by Tony Johnston (Scholastic, 1999). Quilted illustrations adorn this simple story about an apple that falls from a tree. A worm, a bird, and a boy all taste the big red apple. The seeds are dropped and, with rain and sunshine, one becomes a tree with more big red apples. This book is a perfect choice for beginning independent readers. (Planting Reading & Retelling Skills, page 127)

Plants and Trees

The Carrot Seed, by Ruth Krauss (Scholastic, 1974). This is a simple story of perseverance. A little boy plants and nurtures a carrot seed despite his family's belief that nothing will come of it. This is a perfect guided reading story for beginning readers. (Calling All Barbers! page 126)

Counting on the Woods: A Poem, by George Ella Lyon (DK Pub., 1998). The author uses rhyme to count and describe natural objects that are seen in the woods. (A Nature Walk to Count On, page 125; Counting on Seeds, page 125)

Flower Garden, by Eve Bunting (Harcourt Brace Jovanovich, 1994). Simple rhyming text tells of a little girl and her father buying plants at the market. They carry the flowers home where they plant a beautiful window box as a birthday surprise for her mom. (Observation Terrariums, page 116)

The Giving Tree, by Shel Silverstein (HarperCollins, 2003). This is the classic story of friendship between a boy and a tree. The tree gives everything to the boy as he grows older, from apples to branches to trunk and, finally, just a place to rest. (Picture This! page 115)

Growing Vegetable Soup, by Lois Ehlert (Red Wagon Books, 2004). Bold, colorful illustrations make this story about a child and his father growing vegetables to make soup a classroom favorite. (Cooking Vegetable Soup, page 124)

Jamie O'Rourke and the Big Potato: An Irish Folktale, retold and illustrated by Tomie DePaola (Putnam, 1992). This is the tale of a lazy and foolish man who catches a leprechaun and agrees to beging given a potato seed instead of a pot of gold in exchange for the leprechaun's freedom. The fully-grown potato is the largest Jamie's town has ever seen. (A Sweet Idea, page 126)

Old Elm Speaks: Tree Poems, by Kristine O'Connell George (Clarion Books, 1998). The verses describe what trees might think and say to each other and things they do for humans. (Haiku, page 120)

Sky Tree: Seeing Science Through Art, by Thomas Locker with Candace Christiansen (HarperCollins, 1995). With poetic verse and oil paintings, the reader discovers how one tree changes with the seasons. (A Tree for All Seasons, page 123)

Stone Soup, any traditional version. (Cooking Vegetable Soup, page 124)

Sunflower, by Miela Ford (Greenwillow Books, 1995). This story of a little girl planting a sunflower seed is a perfect how-to for children planting a first garden. (Plant Posters, page 122)

Sunflower House, by Eve Bunting (Harcourt Brace & Co., 1996). A little boy plants sunflower seeds in his backyard. He and his friends play in the flowers when they grow tall enough to provide a "roof." Then, at the end of the season, he picks all the seeds when the sunflowers begin to die. (Seed Mosaics, page 123)

Tiny Green Thumbs, by C. Z. Guest (Hyperion Books for Children, 2000). A little rabbit, his grandmother, and a mouse plant a vegetable garden. Step-by-step instructions for growing sunflowers, carrots, beans, corn, and cucumbers are included in this charming story. (Grow Your Own Experiments! page 117)

The Tiny Seed, by Eric Carle (Picture Book Studio, 1990). A seed, tinier than the rest, is carried on a long journey by the wind. Through the seasons, it survives to become a huge flower. (Planting Reading & Retelling Skills, page 127)

Plants and Trees

Additional Suggested Literature

Nonfiction

Growing Colors, by Bruce McMillan (Lothrop, Lee & Shepard Books, 1988). Vivid photographs of vegetables depict nature's colorful bounty.

Red Leaf, Yellow Leaf, by Lois Ehlert (Harcourt Brace Jovanovich, 1991). A child describes how the leaves of a maple tree change through the seasons. A perfect book to introduce young learners to the beauty and mystery of the seasons.

Fiction

Grandpa's Garden Lunch, by Judith Caseley (Greenwillow Books, 1990). A little girl and her grandfather tend a vegetable garden. They reap its rewards by eating the vegetables for a healthy lunch. This book is the perfect tool to introduce a discussion about food groups and meal planning.

Miss Rumphius, by Barbara Cooney (Puffin Books, 1985). As a little girl, Miss Alice Rumphius plans to travel to faraway places, live by the sea, and make the world a more beautiful place. She becomes a much-loved figure in her neighborhood when she spreads the beauty of lupines.

Mrs. Spitzer's Garden, by Edith Pattou (Harcourt, 2001). This book is a must-have for every teacher! The author draws a wonderful and fitting analogy between nurturing a classroom of students and growing a colorful garden with a variety of plants.

Once There Was a Tree, by Natalia Romanova (Dial Books, 1985). Many creatures in the forest are still attracted to an old tree stump, prompting the tree stump to realize that it is still needed.

Planting a Rainbow, by Lois Ehlert (Harcourt, 2003). A young gardener and her mom plant flowers of every color of the rainbow. Labeled illustrations are brightly colored.

Plantpet, by Elise Primavera (G. P. Putnam's Sons, 1994). A gardener cultivates and then nearly loses his beloved pet, a plant. The needs of plants are reviewed in this fictional tale of friendship.

The Story of Johnny Appleseed, by Aliki (Prentice-Hall, 1963). This is a fictional account of John Chapman, known the world over as Johnny Appleseed because he helped a great many pioneers by planting apple seeds.

Tops & Bottoms, adapted by Janet Stevens (Harcourt Brace, 1995). This is a tale of a lazy bear who is outwitted by a clever hare. The rabbit agrees to do all the work in the vegetable garden while splitting the vegetables in half—tops and bottoms. This book has the unique quality of opening top to bottom instead of side to side.

Language Arts

Plants and Trees

Life Cycle Flowchart

Literature: *Pumpkin Circle: The Story of a Garden*, by George Levenson

Materials: Poster board or construction paper, crayons or markers

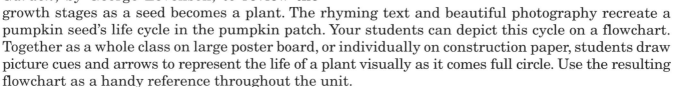

Activity: Read *Pumpkin Circle: The Story of a Garden*, by George Levenson, to review the growth stages as a seed becomes a plant. The rhyming text and beautiful photography recreate a pumpkin seed's life cycle in the pumpkin patch. Your students can depict this cycle on a flowchart. Together as a whole class on large poster board, or individually on construction paper, students draw picture cues and arrows to represent the life of a plant visually as it comes full circle. Use the resulting flowchart as a handy reference throughout the unit.

Story Pies

Literature: *From Seed to Plant*, by Gail Gibbons

Materials: scissors, pencils, construction paper, glue

Activity: Continue practicing sequencing with small-group "story pies" and the easy-to-read information in *From Seed to Plant*, by Gail Gibbons. Give each class member a large construction paper circular shape. Divide the "pie" into even pieces depending on the number of main story events. After cutting out the pie slices, each student will write a simple sentence and create a corresponding illustration that explains the steps from seed to full grown plant—one step on each slice of pie. Students should then reassemble the completed pie slices in sequential order and glue them onto a larger circle. Hang these pies around the classroom for a truly appetizing display!

Picture This!

Literature: *The Giving Tree*, by Shel Silverstein

Materials: Old magazines (pictures of wood products), construction paper, scissors, glue

Activity: After sharing the classic friendship in *The Giving Tree*, by Shel Silverstein, give each pair of students a few old magazines and a large piece of construction paper shaped like a tree or have the children draw a large tree on their papers. Students will use the magazine pictures to make a collage of things that come from trees. Remind students of the products from different parts of the tree that the tree in the story gave to his friend.

© Carson-Dellosa • CD-0584 *Learning through Literature*

Plants and Trees

Take a Hike!

Literature: *The Tremendous Tree Book*, by Barbara Brenner and May Garelick

Materials: Small books for students to wear on strings (see page 118 for directions), pencils, resealable plastic bags

Activity: Use real trees in your school yard or neighborhood and *The Tremendous Tree Book*, by Barbara Brenner and May Garelick, to begin a study of trees. After reading the book's rhyming text aloud, take your students on a hike to observe what they just heard in the story. As the children walk around a specified area, talk about differences and similarities in the types of trees you see. Point out the parts of each tree (trunk, limbs, leaves, and roots) and lead a discussion comparing coniferous and deciduous trees. Students can record observations about how the trees look and feel in small books that are carried around their necks with string. (See page 118 for booklet instructions.)

In the autumn when leaves and twigs are already on the ground, conduct a sampling expedition. Students can pick up fallen leaves, twigs, needles, pinecones, and acorns and keep them safe in small resealable plastic bags.

Extensions: Students can use their recorded observations to create a paragraph about trees. Gather the children in a central location and ask them for sentences about the hike they took. Act as a scribe, writing just what the children say about the topic. The students can then practice reading the paragraph aloud, strengthening both their reading skills and their understanding of trees.

Observation Terrariums

Literature: *Flower Garden*, by Eve Bunting

Materials: Clean, 2-liter soda bottle; craft knife or sturdy scissors; gravel; potting soil; seeds, seedlings, or flowering plants; magnifying glasses; science journals; pencils; water

Activity: *Flower Garden*, by Eve Bunting, is the perfect springboard for planting your own seedlings. A little girl buys beautiful flowers and plants them in a window box for her mother. Imitate the main characters by building a terrarium in a clean soda bottle. Remove the wrapper, cut off the top of the bottle, and set it aside. Place gravel in the bottom and fill partway with soil. Then plant seeds, seedlings, or flowering plants. Water the plants as needed. To keep the soil moist, cover your terrarium with the top of the bottle. Then, place the bottle in a sun-drenched area along with magnifying glasses and science journals for recording observations.

© Carson-Dellosa • CD-0584 *Learning through Literature*

Plants and Trees

Grow Your Own Experiments!

Literature: *Tiny Green Thumbs*, by C. Z. Guest

Materials: Bean seeds, potting soil, peat pots or cardboard egg cartons, old newspapers, journal, pencils

Activity: During this unit your students will certainly be anxious to start planting. Capitalize on that motivation and provide some simple instructions with the story of *Tiny Green Thumbs*, by C. Z. Guest. In it, readers are provided step-by-step instructions as small animals plant a vegetable garden. Begin your own indoor garden that will be perfect for observations and experiments. Use some individual planting cups, such as the small peat pots available at garden centers or even cardboard egg cartons. You will also need bean seeds and soil. (Bean seeds are very quick to germinate which is best for impatient little gardeners!) Break the class into small groups, each of which will create its own learning garden.

You may want to clear one large table to use as a working space. Cover it with newspaper to catch the inevitable spills and lay out an open bag of soil, a bag of beans, all the planting pots, and a small watering can. Rotate the groups through the work station so you or a parent volunteer can supervise the planting.

Each cooperative group should receive several peat pots or one cardboard egg carton for use as planters. Using a pencil, poke a hole in the bottom of each cup for drainage. Fill each cup halfway with soil. Put in a bean seed and cover with soil. Place the garden on a small stack of newspapers in a sunny window. Water a little each day. The newspapers should soak up any excess liquid. In just a few days the seeds are ripe for observation!

Every few days, each group will gently dig up one seed. Observe the seedling and make note of how it has changed. Discuss the current stage of growth, and have the cooperative groups record their observations in a gardening journal using simple sentences and/or illustrations.

Students should look for the following germination stages to occur: 1) the seed coat splits, 2) roots begin to grow, and 3) the seedling sprouts.

Plants and Trees

Booklet Instructions

1. Fold a sheet of copier paper in half lengthwise (see diagram A).

2. Fold the paper in half two more times to divide the sheet into eight sections (see diagrams B and C).

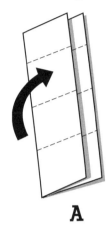

3. Open the folded paper and lay it flat as shown in diagram D. Raise the center fold to form a "tent" shape and then cut along the fold to make a short slit between two panels. See diagram E.

4. Pick up the "tent" and spread apart the center panels to form the booklet. See diagrams F and G.

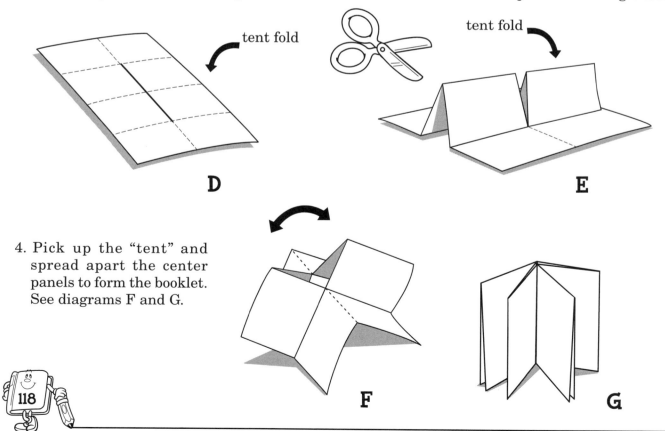

© Carson-Dellosa • CD-0584 *Learning through Literature*

Author Ideas

Plants and Trees

The ABCs of Plants

Literature: *A Gardener's Alphabet*, by Mary Azarian

Materials: Chart paper and marker, paper, pencils, and crayons

Activity: Create your own alphabet book of plant terminology as a fun and informative culminating activity. Brainstorm a list of important plant words and record them on chart paper. Then read aloud *A Gardener's Alphabet*, by Mary Azarian. Did your class learn any new terms that they can add to the chart? Have each student choose a letter of the alphabet (or assign letters, if necessary) and create a page with words and pictures representing that letter. Your students will not only review the unit on plants, but also get good practice in alphabetizing when they put the pages together.

Tree-mendous Books!

Literature: *Tell Me, Tree: All About Trees for Kids*, by Gail Gibbons

Materials: Three sheets of green construction paper per child, small piece of brown construction paper per child, white paper, stapler, scissors, glue, pencils, tree pattern (reproducible, page 121)

Activity: Create a step book in which to record facts learned about trees or the story elements of a picture book. Read *Tell Me, Tree*, by Gail Gibbons, one section at a time. Children can keep track of all the new information about how to identify trees and the parts of trees in their own tree-shaped books.

To make the step book: Transfer an enlarged copy of the tree pattern onto poster board and cut out to make a template. Using the template, trace the tree shape on green construction paper and cut it out. Lay two green sheets of construction paper together. Slide the top piece about 2 in. (5 cm) higher than the bottom piece. Fold both sheets so that each has about 1–2 in. (3–5 cm) margin at the bottom. Staple at the top. Trim the resulting step book so it will look wavy and bushy like a real treetop. Cut the brown paper so it resembles a trunk and glue it to the tree step book. Now your students have a "tree-mendous" place to do some writing!

Plants and Trees

Shape Books

Materials: Materials for making booklets shaped like leaves or trees (patterns on page 128), pencils

Activity: For each student, create a shape book that resembles a leaf. (You may enlarge and copy the leaves on page 128 to make the booklets.) Include blank pages in the booklets for the students to respond to journal topics, such as:

- Types of trees
- Animals that live in trees
- We need trees because . . .
- Products from a tree

Descriptive Writing

Literature: *Autumn Leaves*, by Ken Robbins

Materials: Real autumn leaves, paper and pencils

Activity: After reading *Autumn Leaves*, by Ken Robbins, put your young authors to the test. You will need a variety of autumn leaves for this skill-building activity. Have each child choose a leaf and study it carefully. Encourage the child to write descriptive words describing the size, shape, color, and texture of the leaf. Can the other students match each leaf to the correct paragraph?

Haiku

Literature: *Old Elm Speaks: Tree Poems*, by Kristine O'Connell George

Materials: Chart paper and marker, paper, pencils, materials to make a class book

Activity: Because nature is often the topic of this beautiful form of poetry, now is the perfect time to introduce haiku. Read several poems aloud together from *Old Elm Speaks: Tree Poems*, by Kristine O'Connell George. Chart your favorite haiku and lead your students to recognize the syllabic pattern of 5-7-5. Each child will then write his own haiku about trees or leaves. Brainstorm important words on chart paper. Children can use the resulting chart to arrange 17 wonderful syllables to create an ode to nature. Have students illustrate their final copies and display them for all to admire.

I can hear the wind
Whistling through the old branches
As the leaves float down.

Proud and mighty stands
The oak tree in my backyard,
A tower of strength.

© Carson-Dellosa • CD-0584 *Learning through Literature*

Tree-mendous Books! Pattern

Art, Music & Drama

Singing the Cycle

Literature: *This Is the Sunflower*, by Lola M. Schaefer

Activity: Life cycles of plants are presented in many books for children. The repetitive rhythm of *This Is the Sunflower*, by Lola Schaefer, may make it a classroom favorite. Children love the cumulative pattern and are eager to imitate the beat. Give your students the chance to sing and learn! Sung to the familiar tune of "The Farmer in the Dell," this rhyme reinforces the process of growth. Add exaggerated hand motions to complete the routine!

The gardener plants a seed.
The gardener plants a seed.
Hi ho the seed-e-o!
The gardener plants a seed.

The rain comes splashing down.
The rain comes splashing down.
Hi ho the seed-e-o!
The rain comes splashing down.

Additional verses include:
The root takes a drink . . .
It travels up the stem . . .
The flower starts to bloom . . .

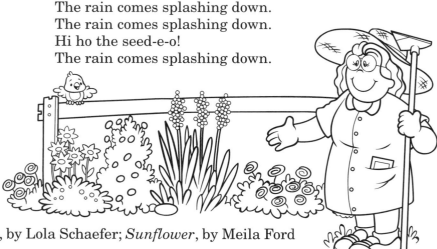

Plant Posters

Literature: *This Is the Sunflower*, by Lola Schaefer; *Sunflower*, by Meila Ford

Materials: Large sheets of construction paper, paint, crayons or markers

Activity: Use a large sunflower, like the one introduced in *This Is the Sunflower*, by Lola Schaefer, or in *Sunflower*, by Meila Ford, to teach the parts of a plant. Have each child paint his own giant sunflower on a large sheet of construction paper. When it is dry, label the roots, stem, petals, and seed. Display these around the room to serve as bright reminders of the parts of a plant.

A Tree-mendous Hotel

Literature: *Cactus Hotel*, by Brenda Z. Guiberson

Materials: Butcher paper, poster paints, paintbrushes, old magazines, scissors, glue

Activity: One important function of trees is to provide a home for many animals. Share *Cactus Hotel*, by Brenda Z. Guiberson, to inspire a lesson about how trees resemble hotels for animals. Next, divide the class into groups of about four students. Provide each group with a large piece of butcher paper and poster paints. Have each group of students paint a large tree showing the roots, trunk, limbs, and leaves. While the paint is drying, students may draw or cut out magazines pictures of animals that live in trees. Students can use glue to place the bugs, birds, squirrels, etc., in the proper spots.

Plants and Trees

Seed Mosaics

Literature: *Sunflower House*, by Eve Bunting

Materials: Sunflower seeds and other seeds, pencil, thin cardboard or poster board, glue

Activity: Use sunflower and a variety of other seeds to create a mosaic art project. Let each student draw a simple shape with pencil and completely cover it with glue. Have the students arrange the seeds in the glue to create one-of-a-kind designs.

As students are creating their mosaics, read to them about the adventures of a young gardener in *Sunflower House*, by Eve Bunting. As his sunflowers die at the end of summer, a little boy picks all of their seeds. Perhaps he will design a mosaic as well!

After the mosaics have had ample time to dry overnight, hang them on a bulletin board.

A Tree for All Seasons

Literature: *Sky Tree: Seeing Science Through Art*, by Thomas Locker

Materials: Large construction paper sheets, crayons or markers, green tissue paper, glue, sponge, paint, cotton balls or mini marshmallows, watercolor paint and brushes

Activity: *Sky Tree: Seeing Science Through Art* is a beautiful book that illustrates with paintings how a tree changes with each season. Encourage children to appreciate the artwork as you share it. Your students can design their own trees in each of the four seasons with this art project. Fold a large piece of construction paper into fourths. (Fold in half once, then once again.) Draw a simple brown tree with bare branches in each panel (or provide copies to paste in), and label one for each season. Now your students may decorate the trees to represent the seasons:

- Winter: Glue small cotton balls or mini marshmallows onto the trees to represent snow on the branches. Add snow to the ground.
- Spring: Use watercolors to depict a soft-looking, budding tree.
- Summer: Wrap squares of green tissue paper (many shades) around the end of a crayon. Dip the end in glue and press it to the branches. Fill the tree with tissue paper to make it leafy and full.
- Fall: Use a small sponge to paint yellow, orange, and red leaves on the tree and ground.

Fun Recipes

Plants and Trees

Eat Dirt!

Materials: New, clean flowerpot; clean artificial flower on a tall stem; 16 oz. (480 mL) tub whipped topping; 4 c. (960 mL) cold milk; 2 boxes of instant chocolate pudding mix; chocolate sandwich cookies, crushed; chewy candy insects and/or worms; serving spoon (or new, clean trowel); serving bowls; spoons; mixing bowl; mixing spoon

Activity: Bring in this tasty surprise as a reward for learning all about plants. Obtain a new, clean flowerpot and an artificial flower on a tall stem.

Make pudding with cold milk according to package directions. Add whipped topping and half of the crushed cookies. Stir until well blended (stir in some of the chewy bug- or worm-shaped candies as well, if desired). Spoon the mixture into the flowerpot. Add remaining crushed cookies and chewy candies to the top of the pot. Lastly, slide the tall stem into the pot. Serve mixture in individual bowls. You might enjoy building the suspense by telling your students that worms eat soil, and we eat vegetables that come from the soil, so perhaps we should give soil a taste. Let the fun continue as they watch you scoop the wet "dirt full of bugs" into cups for tasting! *Bon appétit!*

Variation: You can also use the individual pudding packs or make single servings by pouring pudding into plastic cups, then covering the pudding with chocolate "dirt" and adding chewy candies.

Cooking Vegetable Soup

Literature: *Growing Vegetable Soup*, by Lois Ehlert; *Stone Soup*, any traditional version

Materials: Soup recipe that includes vegetables representing each edible part of a plant, pot, stove, ladle, serving bowls, spoons

Activity: Read about a child and her father growing a vegetable garden in *Growing Vegetable Soup* or share the story of *Stone Soup*. After hearing the story by Lois Ehlert your students might like to eat vegetable soup. Extend their learning with a vegetable feast that reinforces the parts of a plant. After discussing the major parts of a plant, gather vegetables that represent each. For example, carrots, turnips, and rutabagas are roots, potatoes are tubers, celery is a stem, tomatoes are the fruit, and of course, you cannot forget sunflower seeds. (You may want to send home a parent letter to request vegetable donations.) Use your favorite vegetable soup recipe and include as many of these ingredients as you can. What a yummy celebration!

Math

Plants and Trees

A Nature Walk to Count On

Literature: *Counting on the Woods: A Poem*, by George Ella Lyon

Materials: Small book on a string for each student (see page 118), pencils, overhead projector or chart paper, marker

Activity: Begin by reading aloud *Counting on the Woods: A Poem*, by George Ella Lyon. Not only can your mathematicians count along, but they can also review information about forests and trees. Do you have trees and gardens near your school? If so, then lead your class on a nature walk. Before your walk, have each student make a booklet to hang around her neck on a string. (See page 118 for booklet-making directions.) Each student then can record notes (using pictures and numbers) about what she sees on the walk. Use questions like the following to inspire your students:

- How many squirrels are scampering around?
- Are birds singing, building nests, or flying? Can you count them?
- Did someone glimpse a butterfly fluttering by? How many butterflies all together did you count?
- How many points are on an oak leaf?
- How many leaves does a wildflower have?
- How many petals on a daisy?

Once back in the classroom, the students may create a poem using the information they gathered. Model this procedure on the overhead projector or on chart paper. Practice choral reading by reciting the poem several times. The students may wish to create their own counting books, including illustrations. Note: Older students may make this type of counting book for a younger class. Pairs of older children could also use digital cameras to record their trip to the woods, then print the pictures, add text, and bind the pages into a book.

Counting on Seeds

Literature: *Counting on the Woods: A Poem*, by George Ella Lyon

Materials: Large dried sunflower head, paper and pencils

Activity: Practice math skills with a sunflower and *Counting on the Woods*, by George Ella Lyon. Begin by reading this counting book aloud. Not only can your mathematicians count along, but they can also review information about forests and trees. Obtain a large sunflower head and have students estimate how many seeds are contained in the center. Record estimates, then count the actual seeds together. Reward the closest guess. Use the seeds to practice addition and subtraction fact families. Remember to roast some sunflower seeds for a snack!

Plants and Trees

A Sweet Idea

Literature: *Jamie O'Rourke and the Big Potato: An Irish Folktale*, by Tomie dePaola

Materials: Clean jar (mayonnaise size works well), water, fresh sweet potato, toothpicks, ruler or measuring tape, chart paper and marker

Activity: Your students will be excited to see a plant take root. After reading *Jamie O'Rourke and the Big Potato* by Tomie DePaola, they also will be eager to work with potatoes! Jamie is a lazy man who foolishly trades a pot of gold for a potato seed. This magic potato keeps growing and growing! Fill a jar full of water to within an inch (3 cm) of the top. Stick three toothpicks into a sweet potato so you can prop the potato up in the jar. The toothpicks will rest over the top of the jar and allow the sweet potato to sit in the water. In a few days, roots will begin to sprout into the water. Will this potato grow like Jamie's? Choose one student each day or every several days to measure the roots. Record the measurements on a large class chart. The growth chart can then be used to inspire math problems, such as, "Which day saw the most growth?" or, "On how many days did the roots grow at least $1/2$ in. (13 mm)?"

Calling All Barbers!

Literature: *The Carrot Seed*, by Ruth Krauss

Materials: Colored pencils, plastic foam cups, potting soil, grass seed, rulers, paper, pencils, scissors, camera (optional)

Activity: Each student will use colored pencils to decorate a plastic foam cup to look like a face. Fill each cup three-fourths full with soil. Each student may then sprinkle a generous pinch of grass seed on top and cover very lightly with soil. Keep the container watered and place it in a sunny window. In about a week, each student's foam head will have green hair growing. As the class is waiting for the grass to sprout, read *The Carrot Seed*, by Ruth Krauss. In this classic picture book, a little boy waits patiently for his carrot seed to sprout. Challenge your students to be as patient and confident as the main character.

(Note: Young children may find squirting water bottles easier to manage than watering cans. It is a good idea to prepare a few extra cups with soil and grass seed in case a student over-waters and drowns the seeds, spills his cup, or the seeds simply fail to grow.)

Practice measurement skills by having each student use a ruler to measure the grass every few days. Each child can keep track of the growth on his own line graph. When everyone's grass has grown a few inches (several centimeters) tall, transform your classroom into a barbershop and allow students to use scissors to cut the grass "hair." You definitely will want to have a camera on hand as your students give their first haircuts.

At-Home Activities

Plants and Trees

Autumn Leaves Backpack

Literature: *Autumn Leaves*, by Ken Robbins

Materials: Backpack, copy of *Autumn Leaves*, leaves, waxed paper, booklet on a string (see directions on page 118 to make booklet), pencil, crayons

Activity: *Autumn Leaves* is an easy-to-read reference guide for identifying a variety of leaves. It is the perfect companion to activities a student can complete at home. To include families in your unit of study and enlist their support, send home a backpack with the literature book, a direction sheet, and all the supplies necessary to complete the activities. Activity ideas include: collecting leaves that are pressed between sheets of waxed paper with a warm iron and making a booklet about trees and leaves (child takes a walk and records his observations in his booklet).

Planting Reading & Retelling Skills

Literature: *The Big Red Apple*, by Tony Johnston; *The Tiny Seed*, by Eric Carle; *From Seed to Sunflower*, by Gerald Legg

Materials: Backpack, tagboard, construction paper, flower pattern (reproducible, page 128), scissors, glue, pencils and crayons, tape, straws

Activity: Pack a backpack with several garden-related books, enlarged copy of the flower pattern (page 128), construction paper, scissors, glue, drinking straw, and coloring materials. Be sure also to enclose a direction sheet that explains the activity. *The Big Red Apple*, by Tony Johnston; *The Tiny Seed*, by Eric Carle; and *From Seed to Sunflower*, by Gerald Legg, all tell the tale of a seed becoming a plant in an easy-to-read format that is perfect for beginners. At home, the child must choose one story to read. He should read it several times over the next few days: silently to himself, with a parent, to a sibling, etc. When the child is ready for the story-mapping activity, he will complete his flower. To do this, the child glues the flower onto construction paper. On each petal, the child will describe one step in the life cycle of a plant. When finished, he cuts out the flower and affixes it to a drinking straw.

© Carson-Dellosa • CD-0584 *Learning through Literature*

Leaf and Flower Patterns